# Selling the City

# SELLING THE CITY: MARKETING APPROACHES IN PUBLIC SECTOR URBAN PLANNING

## G. J. Ashworth
## and
## H. Voogd

**Belhaven Press**
(a division of Pinter Publishers)
London and New York

© G.J. Ashworth and H. Voogd

First published in Great Britain in 1990 by
Belhaven Press (a division of Pinter Publishers),
25 Floral Street, London WC2E 9DS

**British Library Cataloguing in Publication Data**
A CIP catalogue record for this book is available from the
British Library

ISBN 1 85293 008 X✓

For enquiries in North America please contact
PO Box 197, Irvington, NY 10533

**Library of Congress Cataloging in Publication Data**

A CIP catalog record for this book
is available from the Library of Congress

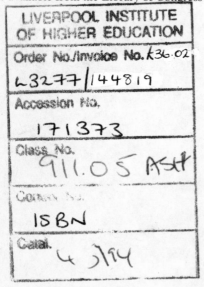
Typeset by Florencetype Ltd, Kewstoke, Avon
Printed and bound by Biddles Ltd, Guildford and Kings Lynn

# Contents

# List of figures

# List of tables

# Preface

It is rarely the appropriate time to write a particular book and this one is no exception. A considered assessment of the application of marketing within public sector urban planning should wait for sufficient practical experience to be accumulated, its effects on planning objectives carefully monitored, so that general lessons about its effectiveness can be drawn. Although the widely reported US city promotions have about a generation's experience, their 'discovery' and import by Western European planners is much more recent and the specialised agencies with specific marketing commissions were mostly established in the course of the 1980s. A critique of the results of their efforts and, probably more significant if less publicised, of the slow seeping of marketing techniques into local authority planning departments, must wait at least ten years.

On the other hand, practitioners in public authorities are now debating the possible role of market planning, speculating about its outcomes and tentatively experimenting with various aspects of it in plans currently being drafted. They require from a university planning department summaries of past experience from wherever that can be gleaned, and a systematic account of the procedures, components and implications of marketing in the particular context of place management for public sector goals. Equally as educators we have the responsibility for equipping those who will very shortly be working within a planning system that has added marketing to its range of techniques and method of defining and solving urban planning problems. They require an understanding of market planning now, how it works, and such skills as necessary to operate it effectively. If this book is to be of maximum assistance to either of these groups, it should ideally have been written ten years ago.

From what has been said above, it is clear that this book has been written for students of planning and for colleagues in planning departments of public authorities and other agencies operating in the public sector. We are aware that any attempt to bridge ideas originating from different academic disciplines takes the inevitable risk of falling between them. But the potential gains to be made by incorporating new ideas make this risk worth taking.

This book is not written for marketing specialists, who will find little new in theory or concepts even though these appear in what are likely to be unfamiliar political and spatial contexts. Similarly colleagues in other academic disciplines studying the city, particularly those concerned with urban public administration, the perception and promotion of urban images and many aspects of the management of behaviour in cities, will be familiar with some of the material and cases we discuss but not necessarily with the perspectives through which we discuss them.

The examples used as the basis of the experience upon which this book rests are derived from two sources: the descriptions and analysis of others as presented in the accessible literature, and our own practical experience of managing the construction of commissioned planning studies mostly for local authorities. Both sources are necessarily limited, not least in terms of their spatial distribution, with cases from North America being dominant in the literature and our own experience being principally in North Western Europe.

It is argued later that few of those actually engaged in market planning can find the time to write about it. This has proved true equally for the authors and Iain Stevenson of Pinters has demonstrated unusual patience. Our dedication must be to those currently struggling with the attempt to find solutions to urban planning problems, and to those soon to join them in that struggle. This is our market and the only way to assess the value of our product is the extent to which it serves it.

GJA
HV
University of
Groningen

# 1 Cities and markets

Public authorities in recent years have demonstrated a changing attitude towards the role of public planning. If we consider urban policies in, for instance, France, the United Kingdom or the Netherlands, then an increasing role for private sector led initiatives and simultaneously a reduction in government control and financial support for such projects is noticeable. In seeking solutions to long-standing urban problems, such as inner city revitalisation, there is a growing interest in various forms of co-operation between public and private interests, responsibilities and finance. The relevance of such market orientation may seem rather obvious in countries like the USA, which traditionally have a decentralised, more liberal planning system 'dominated by working class realists with a low regard for missionaries' (cf. Dyckman, 1961). But even in countries with quite different planning histories, it certainly provides new perspectives for city planning in general and the management of such facilities as housing and public transport, infrastructural provision for which is still financed and regulated by governments.

At its simplest level this is just the recognition that many urban activities, such as housing, employment and recreation, operate within a 'market' whether explicit or not, and the operation of such markets have important effects upon each other. However, the adoption of a more market-oriented urban planning implies a substitution of an approach from the ordering of space and its organisation by a closer attention to the wishes and needs of actual or potential users. The implications of this shift from a supply side to a demand side orientation is the substance of this book. First, this chapter will endeavour to define more closely the changing context of cities and city planning.

## Recent urban change

Contemporary interest in the juxtaposition of cities and markets stems essentially from changes in both the character of the city, at least in

Western societies, together with changes in the attitudes of governments, both national and local, to these changes.

It can reasonably be argued that cities have always existed within markets of one sort or another, both in the sense that they compete with others for resources, activities, residents and the attention of outsiders, and equally in the sense that each service offered within the city competes with others for users or consumers. However, the justification for this book at this time rests upon the contention that a particular set of recent and related urban developments have provoked or encouraged a reaction among those responsible for urban planning and management at various levels in the public sector that has reappraised the relationship between cities and markets.

These changes have been variously listed and explained as part of more general theories encapsulated in titles such as advanced capitalism (Harvey, 1989), post-industrialism (Lever, 1987) or post-modernism (Cooke, 1987; Harvey, 1988; Short, 1989). Despite differences in emphasis in these explanations, there is a broad unanimity that a series of fundamental shifts in western economics have become particularly apparant in the last few decades which have altered the nature of urban economies in particular and consequently the way cities are used. These can be cursorily summarised as:

1.  The shift in what is produced, namely the de–industrialisation of cities and the rise in importance of not only services in general but the higher order personal quaternary services in particular which satisfy the individual's needs for entertainment, education, culture and the like.
2.  The organisational changes in how goods and services are produced which have blurred the distinction between public provision for social goals and private production for individual profit and even between the function of cities as centres of production and of collective consumption (Pinch, 1985).
3.  Finally the most important change in where these are produced is the increasing freedom of activities to locate without constraints imposed by the friction of physical distance. It is not that commercial activities have become completely footloose and thus indifferent to the qualities of particular locations; on the contrary the decline in the importance of material transport, the increasing mobility of labour, and the internationalisation of markets has allowed a new set of local place attributes and new definitions of the accessibility of places to become prominent locational determinants.

These changes in the economic functioning of cities can be related to concomitant changes in the relationships of the individual to work, to household structures, to consumption patterns, residential choices and much besides (see Walmesley (1988) for an account of many aspects of the relationship between the individual and modern urban living). For whatever reason urban societies have become more variegated, individualistic, internationally aware, and oriented to life styles based upon a fashion-conscious and rapidly shifting consumerism.

It is not necessary for our purposes to inventorise, explain, justify or theorise about these shifts, nor to determine whether they are part of a long-term transition between historical epochs, or just the continuing evolution of western capitalist democracies along predictable lines. All that is important here is the realisation that they have thrust cities into a new relationship with external and internal markets presenting simultaneously both threats and opportunities. There are inevitably winners and losers both in terms of favoured and disfavoured cities, and equally between particular social and economic groups and individuals within cities. This is in itself hardly new; throughout urban history circumstances have endowed cities and their citizens unequally. The novelty and much of the explanation of the problem is just that the rules of the competitive struggle have been changed quite abruptly; cities, and activities within cities, established upon one set of criteria have found that these no longer confer advantage and quite different valuations are now placed upon urban attributes.

In particular two urban characteristics have become of crucial significance. The first can be grouped under the term amenity which includes an appreciation of quality in the natural or built environment of cities. It is necessarily difficult to define or measure a set of qualities, which may encompass aspects of urban site, the physical characteristics of air, sound and smell, place symbolisms and associations, and architectural and morphological patterns of buildings and spaces. Even more broadly defined it often includes access to a wide collection of urban residential, social, recreational and cultural services whether provided individually or collectively, by public or private enterprises. But, however vaguely delimited, it is clear that such attributes which were once seen as being at best a marginal consideration for the location of economic activities, and at worst an accepted consequence of such activities, are now active determinants in attracting or repelling the location of such activities.

Second, the way cities are now valued as places in which to live, work, recreate or invest makes the way they are viewed of critical significance. The perception of cities, and the mental image held of them, become active components of economic success or failure.

Thus, for whatever reasons, cities have been placed in new competitive situations within which their strengths and weaknesses are quite differently determined than was formally the case. That this has become apparent sooner and with more dramatic consequences in some cities or in some national urban systems than others is evident, but does not detract from our contention that this relationship of cities and markets is in essence new, applicable to cities of a wide range of sizes, economic structures, cultural contexts, and locations, and international in its incidence.

## The city in a competitive world

Before examining the reactions of public planning to these shifts, four cases of the variety of competitive situations in which cities have found themselves, can be reviewed. These indicate both the growing appreciation of the existence of cities in various sorts of markets and the role of the new locational attributes and urban qualities discussed above, in the conduct of such competition.

### Popularity leagues

The publication of popularity league tables of major cities constructed from popular reactions to various attributes, such as perceived residential desirability, environmental quality, or personal safety has long been practised in the United States (e.g. Eisenberg and Englander, 1987; Leven and Stover, 1989). The results of these ratings (such as provided, for example by the Rand-McNally Almanac or the Sierra Magazine) are weighted and publicised with the sort of attention otherwise devoted to national sporting events. In this case public authorities are noting existing national city images and responding with promotion, including often public relations exercises aimed at the compilers of such listings.

### Image and branch office location

At a more specialised level the increasing internationalisation of both production and consumption has awakened cities to the gains to be made by acting as locations for facilities, whether public or private, operating on international markets, which in turn has generated considerable research into the factors that confer such attractions. Typical of such work is that of Dunning and Norman (1987) which simply listed the weightings attributed by decision-makers to particular urban characteristics in influencing the choice of location of branch plants of multinational corporations. Factors such as suitability of the local urban image to the company, local cultural and even linguistic characteristics were weighted the highest, closely followed by sets of local amenities and facilities for health, education, housing and the like. Such more traditionally considered attributes as local financial support, land cost and availability and even local labour were weighted much less highly (see also Sierra Magazine, 1986). Here the markets are more specific to particular users and planning reactions include not only promotion but improvement of specific amenity attributes, many of which can be influenced by local planning action.

*International league tables*

A much wider-ranging and ambitious attempt to describe competition between cities on a continental scale has been attempted by the Datar agency of the French government (**DATAR**, 1989; Gault, 1989). The objective was to score cities according to a range of indices including: ability to attract multinational firms and governmental agencies operating on an international market, centrality in transport and communications networks, importance of research and development, financial institutions, international fairs and congresses, and a wide range of cultural outputs. In this way it could thus be revealed which cities were in fact competing within which arenas for the assumed enormous economic benefits accruing as a consequence of their possession of these various qualities. A clearly implied consequence was the identification of potential winners and losers and the taking of national planning action to strengthen the competitive position of French towns in this respect. Three sorts of results emerged (Table 1.1). First, the delimitation of a number of separate markets such as 'the culture market', 'the international finance market', 'the international passenger transport market' and the like, which although often overlapping had nevertheless their own distinctive characteristics and participating competing cities. Second, various separate 'leagues' of cities could be identified within which competition was fierce but which tended not to compete with each other. There was, for example, a 'capital of Europe' struggle (London, Paris), a 'first division' of such towns as Milan, Rome, Amsterdam, Brussels, Frankfurt, Munich, Madrid and Barcelona competing among themselves, a 'second division', with competitors such as Vienna or Zurich, and so on down lower 'divisions' of regional centres. Third, and perhaps most profitable from the point of view of planning, 'residuals' were highlighted, that is cities with positions in particular markets that were higher or lower than might be expected from their population totals. The 'negative residuals', for example, included such categories as the 'incomplete national capitals' (Berlin, Vienna, Lisbon, Athens), 'overshadowed' towns (Rouen, Saragoza), or 'over-industrial towns' (Liverpool, Essen, Liège). The accuracy of the quantitative scores is not so important as the production of such tables at all, the realisation of the existence of this sort of competition, and the importance attached to it by governments.

Here the city is conceived of as competing within a specified continental market, although in a sense as a national representative opposing other national representative cities, with the implied support of national governments through key infrastructural improvements in the national interest.

*A national plan for international competition*

At the national level the attention paid to the international competitive situation of representative cities is most clearly illustrated by the Dutch

**Table 1.1**   A classification of European cities (after Gault, 1989)

| | |
|---|---|
| 'Capital of Europe' | London (83),  Paris(81) |
| 'Top League' | Milan(70),  Madrid(66),  Munich(65),  Frankfurt(65), Rome(64),  Brussels(64),  Barcelona(64), Amsterdam(63) |
| 'Second League' | Manchester(58),  Berlin(57),  Hamburg(57), Stuttgart(56),  Copenhagen(56),  Athens(56), Rotterdam(55),  Zurich(54),  Turin(54),  Lyons(53), Geneva(52) |
| 'Third League' | Birmingham(51),  Cologne(51),  Lisbon(51), Glasgow(50),  Vienna(49),  Edinburgh(49), Marseilles(48),  Naples(47),  Seville(46),  Strasbourg(46), Basle(45),  Venice(45),  Utrecht(45),  Dusseldorf(44), Florence(44),  Bologna(44),  The Hague(44), Antwerp(44),  Toulouse(44),  Valence(43) |

Fourth National Physical Plan (RPD, 1988). This influential planning policy document both established a general tone of planning principles and also the main lines of a national planning strategy, for the guidance of the subordinate local authorities in the production of their regional and local plans. In sharp contrast to its three predecessors, this 'Fourth Report' concentrated upon the stimulation of economic growth rather than directing its spatial distribution and mitigating its undesirable consequences. Specifically it concerned itself with analysing the competitive situation of the complex of western Dutch cities within Europe and the means by which planning policies could enhance the advantages of these cities especially in the fiercer competitive situation expected in the post–1992 single European market.

Here the realisation of market position extended to more than an analysis of the existing competitive league, as in the French study, and identification of the factors contributing to current strengths and weaknesses of individual Dutch cities in attracting international activities, as in the industrial location studies of individual Dutch cities, it proceeded to outline interventionist strategies for influencing this situation through the public planning system.

## Changing planning perspectives

The changes in the nature of urban economies outlined above, and their consequences for the valuation placed upon urban attributes, need not necessarily have resulted in any particular planning reaction. They have coincided, however, with changes in thinking about public planning that have encouraged planning authorities to react to urban change by intervention in markets. But this introduction of marketing can only by discussed in contrast to more traditional methodologies of urban and regional planning, thereby placing it in its conceptual and methodological context. This section therefore presents briefly an historical perspective of urban planning as a whole, so that the distinctive methods and objectives of concern in this book can be revealed.

The change of thinking about public planning cannot be seen separately from the shift of appreciation for the role of government in the last decade. After the Second World War there were high expectations in most European countries with respect to the guidance by the government of social processes (e.g. see Burtenshaw *et al.*, 1981). These expectations were fed by the fact that public authorities were really able to exercise considerable influence by their own investments in a number of areas such as housing, road planning and welfare facilities. The period of post-war reconstruction of Europe effectively launched public planning as the instrument for the creation of a 'New Jerusalem'. The Second World War created in Europe the necessity for urban reconstruction on a scale that could only be handled by public agencies, together with a popular demand for such intervention, a political will to attempt it and a faith that it could succeed.

The processes of urban development and change, together with their spillover effects, were thus controlled by a constantly growing system of planning procedures, laws and regulations initiated in most countries in the late 1940s and 1950s, but elaborated and refined in the light of experience during the 1960s and 1970s. The system was operated by an equally rapidly increasing professionalised bureaucracy. This expanding complexity resulted, probably inevitably, in inefficiencies, manifested through the delays involved by increasingly complex procedures, failures to co-ordinate between authorities and departments, and a perception that public planning had become inflexible in its operations. Attempts to introduce more responsiveness into the system through participation and other procedures were undertaken almost everywhere, but in practice frequently only increased the complexity of the process (e.g. see Langenieux-Villard, 1985). As a consequence, in the 1970s public planning in several European welfare states was subject to increasing criticism both from within and outside the system (see Ashworth and Voogd, 1988).

This increasing dissatisfaction was in part the result of the disillusion of a generation's experience, rendered probably inevitable by the high expectations. Urban planning problems, whether in social housing, transport, public service provision, or the environment, were not perceived to have been solved. The fact that much had been achieved, that standards of quality had constantly risen in the face of increasing demands made upon the city, and that many of the expectations of the efficacy of the planning system in dealing with intractable problems were in many instances over-confident, could not detract from an ill-defined feeling of unease in many Western European countries that the public planning system had failed. This disillusionment coincided with economic recession in the late 1970s and early 1980s, which had two consequences. First, a planning system that had been designed to constrain, control and direct demands upon urban space, was nonplussed by the failure of those demands and was structurally ill-suited to stimulating, attracting and enhancing them. Second, the problem was compounded by the imposition of heavy budgetary constraints on public expenditure by national governments as a political reaction to economic circumstances in a number of Western European countries. This had a particular effect upon local government expenditures, local revenue possibilities, and the use of the expenditures of national government agencies for local planning purposes. Local planners, disillusioned about the efficacy of traditional practices, and politicians searching for new possibilities for finance, were both open to the suggestion of a new approach.

There is obviously an intimate relation between what is expected of the public planning system and the political climate of opinion (Saunders, 1986; Friedmann, 1989). Local urban planners operate closely in association with the local political state, within the wider constraints imposed with varying degrees of effectiveness by central governments and even more widely within the limits imposed by popular political opinion which largely defines the problems that planning is expected to solve and the instruments that can be employed for that purpose. However, despite this multifaceted relationship caution must be exercised in equating the party political label of a national or local government and a particular approach to urban planning problems. The introduction of more market-oriented approaches was strongly advocated by 'right wing' political parties, which assumed power at the national level in a number of countries by the end of the 1970s (such as the Thatcher administration in the UK) or beginning of the 1980s (the Reagan administration in the US), which showed great interest for political-ideological reasons in bringing back 'the market' into the city (Jossip *et al.*, 1987; Weiss, 1989). Table 1.2 summarises differences in political approach to urban regeneration in England and very similar tables could be constructed for a number of other countries. However, market planning examples can also be found in countries with 'left' oriented national governments or coalitions (France, Spain) and at the urban level it is difficult to trace a correlation between the extent of penetration of market ideas and the political complexion of a particular local authority.

Running parallel to these economic and political developments was an evolution in thinking about the techniques and instruments of urban planning. In the 1950s and 1960s planning practitioners were still concerned with giving direction to the long-range development of the community by

**Table 1.2** Differences in party political approaches to urban regeneration in England since 1979 (after Benington, 1986)

| Conservative central government approaches since 1979 | 'New Left' Labour local approaches 1981–6 |
|---|---|
| Focus on private sector as motor for economic development | Focus on public sector as stimulus for economic change |
| Public land-use planning seen as hindrance to development. Aims at reducing planning controls | Lack of socially responsible planning seen as cause of economic decline |
| Priority to inward investment | Priority to defence of indigenous industries |
| Focus on market | Focus on production |
| Open up local government to market forces | Open up local government to 'popular planning' |

means of 'blueprint' comprehensive plans. In those days urban planning was highly substantive and design-oriented. This provoked a growing disenchantment among many commentators with this traditional approach (e.g. see Faludi, 1973). Manifestations of the dissatisfaction with 'blueprint' planning have taken at least three major lines. First, efforts to make planning more responsive to the needs of clients and decision-makers (e.g. Davidoff, 1965; Friedmann, 1973), which raised a wide-ranging debate on the role of public planning in democratic societies; second, efforts to improve planning through changes to its methods and techniques (e.g. Friend and Jessop, 1969; Voogd, 1983; Dutton and Kraemer, 1985; Wyatt, 1989); and third, efforts to improve planning as an administrative task (e.g. see Wildavsky, 1964; Pressman and Wildavsky, 1973; Gilbert and Specht, 1977; Muller and Needham, 1989).

These, and many other, reactions to the shortcomings of traditional blueprint planning emphasise the process character of public decision-making. The work of the British 'IOR School' (e.g. see Hickling, 1974; Friend *et al.*, 1974) received particular attention in this respect and it inspired, among others, Faludi (1987) to develop a 'decision-centred view' of planning. In his view planning is co-ordinating decisions by making them form a coherent pattern. In accordance with the ideas of the 'IOR School', plans are seen as 'commitment packages' which should stimulate certain identified actors to further action along predictable and desirable lines. From this perspective the goal of urban planning is no longer a well-organised and liveable urban space but a well-organised public decision-making system (see Faludi, 1987, p.128) from which various spatial and other goals will ultimately and inevitably emerge. However, in practice both kinds of goals may very well coincide, for instance through the assessment of equity effects of potential decisions in planning evaluation (see Miller, 1985, 1990).

The current interest in a more marketing-oriented approach to urban planning suggests to some extent a return to the substantive plans of the 1950s and 1960s: physical plans again include promising full-coloured maps that convince the reader that the situation in 10 or 20 years' time will be highly improved. In contrast to the traditional plans, these market-oriented plans do not specifically aim at implementation but more at stimulation of the involvement of specific social groups in the planning process. As such, market planning draws also on some of the ideas of the 'action-oriented' view of planning (Muller and Needham, 1989). However, it also implies a shift in modes of thought. For instance, market planning focuses on target groups and competition instead of interest groups and co-ordination. Market planning not only involves the development and implementation of organisational and spatial-functional strategies, but also of promotional strategies. All these will be elaborated in detail in later chapters, but it is noted here that market planning can be seen as a continuation of a number of long-standing trends within planning practice rather than a completely new departure.

## Towards market planning

For the reasons argued above public authorities in a number of countries in Western Europe have in recent years adopted a distinctly different attitude towards the role of markets within public planning. A succinct means of describing the very varied results of this new attitude and the policies, structures, instruments and practices stemming from it is *city marketing*, a phrase with a long history of use in the United States but which was ascribed a wider set of meanings in Western Europe in the course of the 1980s.

The major difficulty of definition is that the words have been used to include a wide variety of quite different activities with little unanimity of usage emerging. To many commentators in the early 1980s the term meant promotion, or even more narrowly the advertising of the city as a whole (van Gent, 1984; Peelen, 1987); a restriction in meaning which remains dominant in North American practice, where it is more usually found in the literature of marketing than of planning. Others have defined it as one aspect of city management, rather than an alternative form of it (Nelissen, 1989). Most existing definitions are either too narrow or too broad to be useful for our purposes. On the one hand some have written of city marketing as if it were only a set of instruments and strategies (e.g. Nott, 1984; Bartels and Timmer, 1987); one technique among the many possible for exercising planning control. On the other hand others have treated it as a portmanteau description encompassing almost any relationship between public planning authorities and the private sector (see the wide ranging contributions included in Nelissen, 1989 and in Buursink and Borchert, 1987). Certainly an important and well-publicised aspect of the introduction of this new perspective on the public sector management of cities has been reflected in the urban policy initiatives of countries such as France, the United Kingdom, Belgium and the Netherlands, in the course of the 1980s. These all attempted in various ways to define a new relationship with the private sector, through both experiments with new organisational forms, and a larger dependence upon private investments for the execution of public planning initiatives. In either event city marketing was being defined as an awareness of the advantages of obtaining private investment and the shaping of partnership structures to achieve this (e.g. see Pumain, 1989).

City marketing will be treated here as a process whereby urban activities are as closely as possible related to the demands of targeted customers so as to maximise the efficient social and economic functioning of the area concerned in accordance with whatever goals have been established. These ideas can be logically applied at many spatial scales and thus city marketing can be viewed as a part of broader *geographical marketing* alongside regional or even national marketing. However, the bulk of recent experience concerns specifically the use of marketing approaches as a solution to urban planning problems, hence the focus of this book.

This broad working definition of the marketing of space and spatial qualities encompasses all the various definitions outlined above but proceeds further than most and seeks a more general context within which they can be incorporated. It certainly implies much more than a fashionable terminology and city promotion through four-colour leaflets. Numerous urban activities operate within a market whose objective is the bringing together of supply and demand. The efficient functioning of cities depends essentially upon the efficiency of their operations, including their competitive positions, within such markets (see also Hawes *et al.*, 1985).

In theory all activities have a user, whether regarded as customer, client or recipient, and thus all operate within markets, whether consciously or not, and whether or not the activities are directly priced, managed by public authorities, or undertaken for objectives other than directly attributed financial profit (Kotler, 1972). The urban markets for housing, recreation and many other services are just as much real markets as those for commercial capital investment and their functioning may be as significant for the economic prosperity of a local authority.

Obviously an inefficiently operating housing, education or health service market will have a direct negative effect on the total urban production system. An oversupply of such facilities in relation to demand is clearly wasteful of scarce public resources and may even damage the environment, while an undersupply of such facilities as housing, schools, publicly provided health or recreation facilities is, at the very least, a disincentive to new exogenous investment.

In general terms, there are several types of possible planning intervention in the operation of markets, if they are failing to meet collective objectives, e.g.:

(a) the provision of information relating to an area as a whole to create or strengthen an image in support of private developments;
(b) the provision of a stimulus through development and the improvement of identified elements of the economic and environmental infrastructure;
(c) the regulation of development to prevent urban functions becoming self-damaging in the longer run as a result of the misuse of critical resources in the short term;
(d) the regulation of the urban system in the interests of social groups whose market position is intrinsically weak;
(e) the regulation of development towards longer-term goals than are included within market processes.

Market planning implies that central or local governments not only may but must intervene in selected markets in various ways, so as, for example, to provide the infrastructural framework necessary for private developments to operate profitably which cannot be provided by such developments, and also to ensure that such developments do not become self-defeating by destroying the assets on which they are founded. Essentially, market planning involves procedures and strategies through which urban space is adapted as far as possible to accord with the wishes of selected target groups with the objective of creating the conditions for the efficient operation of the social and economic functions and activities of the area concerned, according to collectively established goals.

In urban market planning spatial policy is inseparably linked with city marketing and especially through the physical structure plan which is largely instrumental in determining the dimensions of the future 'product'. The expectations and approaches of physical planning, therefore, form an important link between city marketing and spatial policy as a whole (see also Ashworth and Voogd, 1988). Dutch planning practice teaches that there is a fundamental difference in orientation between traditional urban planning and a market planning approach (Voogd, 1989a). Traditional physical planning is mostly to a considerable degree 'supply-oriented', i.e. the attention is usually focused on investigating the constraints and physical possibilities ('design') of the existing built environment. The 'demand-side' is often considered as a deduced phenomenon that is usually only treated in daily planning practice in terms of goals and objectives and not as an analytical subject structuring the treatment of the built environment.

PHYSICAL DELIVERY SYSTEM          VALUE DELIVERY SYSTEM

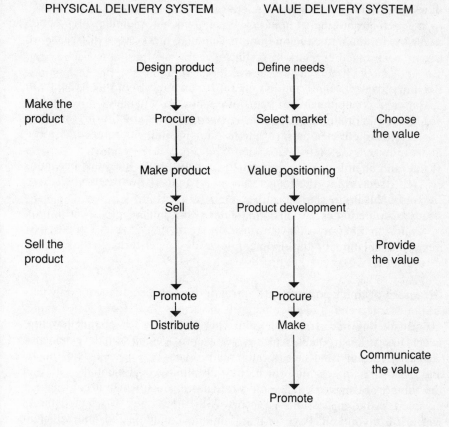

**Figure 1.1**   *Characteristics of a value delivery system*

Market planning, however, is much more 'demand-oriented', i.e. the city and possible changes in the urban facility structure are considered from the perspective of the actual and potential consumers or target groups. It is far more directly goal-oriented linking the professionalism of the managers with the users and potential users of the planned product. The 'interest groups' of conventional planning are replaced by 'customers', which implies a different relationship. In marketing science terms this would be expressed as the difference between a production system based on 'product delivery' and on 'value delivery' (Figure 1.1), and the fact that in public planning the 'product' may be an urban attribute or public service, and the 'value' is some collective rather than individual benefit makes little difference to this argument.

An important task in market planning is to inform the consumers about the 'supply-side' and to invite them to make use, or more or different use, of it. Such promotion is not only relevant in most public services but necessary for their efficient operation. There are other subtle differences of accent that together mark a distinct break with past approaches and implicitly allow, if not encourage, the application of marketing techniques. The important management instrument for the control of functional land-use change is supplemented by a more positive encouragement of the desirable rather than the prevention of the undesirable. The pursuit of such policies leads directly to the shaping and projection of suitable urban images through the built environment and similarly the removal of aspects of the built environment which contribute towards negative images of the city (e.g. see Ashworth, 1988; Neven and Houston, 1980). In this way conventional urban spatial management by its control, for example, of street furniture, landscaping, building design, and many other contributors to what can be termed style, is operating within a new and broader management context of marketing.

## Structure of this book

City marketing has grown out of marketing science, a parent discipline which has at least 50 years of academic development behind it, for the reasons argued above. The theoretical and conceptual relationships between city marketing and the more widely applicable commercial marketing are the subject of Chapter 2. Chapter 3 provides the central process model of how city marketing can be made to work and the essential elements of which it is composed. Each of these components is then treated in more detail, with Chapter 4 being devoted to an analysis of the market and Chapter 5 to that of the product, answering the questions to whom and what is to be marketed respectively. Market and product are brought into conjunction through various marketing strategies and marketing methods. The promotion of place images is in practice central to these methods. This is treated in Chapter 6 from the point of view of the individual's reception and transmission of images, and in Chapter 7 from the viewpoint of deliberate, goal–directed image building as part of promotional exercises. A central argument of this book is that the use of city marketing approaches implies more than the simple adoption of a new instrument, it requires equally the adoption of appropriate organisational structures and working methods. The interrelationships between the marketing methods and the organisational forms is a central theme of Chapter 8, which examines in more detail some case studies of marketing applications, particularly selected from North American and Western European experience.

Finally an assessment, necessarily tentative given the still limited and varied experiences of practical application, is made. A preliminary balance sheet of strengths and weaknesses, successes and failures is attempted, if only to point the way towards more effective uses of the approach, within a broad range of public authorities in pursuit of a variety of goals in the near future.

# 2 Marketing theory and place marketing

## Applying marketing theory

Despite the recognition in public as well as private organisations that a more consumer-oriented approach is desirable, there remains a substantial gap between the crystallisation of these attitudes towards the role of markets and the development of a set of directly relevant concepts which can underpin the construction of a series of practical procedures for the marketing of places. A vague sense of unease that markets are being neglected and the consequent import of a new set of procedural techniques, or worse still a new terminology to describe existing practices, is not enough. A framework of concepts must be borrowed or developed from theory to bridge this gap in application.

Two sorts of reactions to this task are prevalent, neither of which advances the arguments proposed here, but both of which can be discovered with ease in both the analytical literature and among practitioners and thus cannot be ignored.

The first could be labelled 'naive simplification'. This view would regard this chapter as unnecessary and possibly obscurantist as the recognition that organisations operate within markets is so self-evident as to render unnecessary any further conceptualisation and that the procedures and techniques have long existed. The task is therefore simply one of direct transference to the marketing of places of the skills, methods and personnel already well practised in the marketing of other goods and services. Further research is largely therefore a matter of detail such as the monitoring of the use and effectiveness of these transferred instruments and procedures. Such work could be labelled technical rather than conceptual and would include many studies of organisational structures (see the comparative case studies in Klaassen *et al.*, 1989), choices of promotional media (van Doorn, 1986; van Gent, 1984) or even what amounts to the drawing up of a quantitative league table of local authority expenditures as a measure of participation (Bartels and Timmer, 1987). Among practitioners this view is manifest in the belief that place is a product like any other in this respect, to be marketed in the same way with the same instruments. A frequently implied concomitant is that all promotion must to a greater or lesser degree be furthering the product in the market, and is therefore to be encouraged rather than monitored.

A quite different and seemingly contradictory reaction which takes realism to the point of despair is the belief that the marketing of places is so insubstantial an idea as to be well beyond current competence, and that the 'state of the art' can be dismissed as little more than the distribution of a few laudatory brochures or seaside resort town guides, which hardly constitutes professional marketing. As late as 1984, van Gent was still expressing a *cri de coeur* in an article entitled 'city marketing' or 'what business are we in?'; in 1986 Andriesse subtitled an article on city marketing in a principal national marketing journal, as 'an unexplored area' in which was introduced the 'vague' and 'unknown concept' of city marketing. In other and less dismissive words, there is a widespread belief that place marketing has advanced little further than a slogan of the 'I love New York' variety and that much of the practice was based on very dubious theoretical premises.

It is the contention of this chapter that neither extreme position is an accurate reflection of either best contemporary practice nor attainable near future possibilities. The selling of places within a market can and must be related to a set of basic concepts rooted principally in marketing science which recognise and largely accommodate the distinctive characteristics of places as products and that consequently an equally distinctive practice is in the process of developing its particular techniques. The purpose of this chapter is to outline such concepts.

*The basic concepts*

The generally accepted definitions of the nature and scope of marketing neither explicitly include the possibility of place marketing nor deliberately exclude it, but like many such definitions are both innocuous and not very helpful for our purposes. To define marketing as we have suggested in the previous chapter as a 'customer-oriented approach' or the 'exchange principle' ('exchange is a central concept in marketing and may well serve as the foundation for that elusive general theory of marketing' Lovelock and Weinberg, 1984) correctly identifies various important foci. Equally such definitions as 'marketing is a process of planning and movement of a product from the supplier to those who are to use it . . . and the marketing process is incomplete unless all of its functions are performed' (Kotler, 1986), are more encompassing, while even more comprehensive is the checklist that marketing includes an approach to commodities, to institutions, to functions, to management, and ultimately to society. These do not in themselves confront the particular difficulties inherent in place marketing.

These difficulties can be grouped under two main headings, viz. those relating to the peculiarities of places as marketable products and those stemming from the goals of place marketing. Places are obviously different from many other products offered on the market both in the composite nature of the product and the way it is used by the customer. The selling of a place is not the transfer of rights of ownership but only of limited and generally non-exclusive rights of use. The second kind of difficulty lies in the differences in objective between organisations marketing places and those engaged in most marketing of goods and services (see Nott, 1984). The existence of both areas of difficulty can be conceded as more or less self-evident: the relevant question is whether they can be included comfortably within a marketing approach. It is our contention that concepts can be developed which when taken together allow this to occur.

*Marketing in non-profit organisations* The rather clumsily expressed negative term, *marketing in non-profit organisations*, sometimes equally awkwardly found as *marketing in non-business organisations*, is an attempt to address the problem of goals, and can be traced back to the seminal work of Kotler and Levy in 1969. The assumption is that places are generally marketed by public or semi-public agencies whereas marketing was at least originally developed to serve the requirements of private firms and that the objectives of the two sorts of organisations are necessarily fundamentally different. This difference has been assessed by some (for example, Gaedeke, 1977), and more recently Hommes and Geraads (1984) as so wide as to deny the very possibility of place marketing. Neither assumption is necessarily always correct, but this is no solution to the central problem that those who usually market places have goals other than a direct financial profit for the organisation conducting the marketing. Some have claimed that this in itself renders the marketing approach invalid either because the absence of a direct financial nexus between customer and firm renders marketing impossible to monitor (Fines, 1981) or because the attempt to create such a relationship will so distort the objectives of public authorities that they will cease to operate in the public sector in all but name.

In answer it can be reiterated that all organisations cannot fail to operate within markets, whether consciously or not; even public utility monopolies allow customers the choice of the amount of patronage or even whether to abstain completely in favour of alternative expenditures. The different nature of 'non-business' goals merely determines that a primary task is to determine the nature of those markets and of those customers, however differently named. In addition Fines's (1981) insistence on the maintenance of what he terms 'the exchange concept' is not necessarily denied if that exchange is non-monetary or indirect. This is in itself, however, an incomplete answer to an incompletely formulated set of questions. The concept of marketing for non-profit organisations as developed by Kotler and Zaltman (1971), Kotler (1982), and Lovelock and Weinberg (1984) incorporates the broader and longer-term goals of public authorities and accommodates the absence of a direct financial link between producer and consumer through an extension of the concept of what constitutes a market. As Capon (1981) has argued the obvious differences of objectives leads to an equally obvious different set of marketing strategies, not to a rejection of marketing as such.

*Social marketing* The concept of *social* (or societal) *marketing* was introduced in the early 1970s (see Kotler and Zaltman, 1971; Lazer and Kelley, 1973; Rados, 1981) to accommodate a number of distinctly different trends which need to be distinguished. One usage is marketing that 'is aimed at enhancing the consumer's and society's wellbeing' (Kotler, 1986, p.16), including over the longer as well as immediate term. This could be dismissed as either little more than a defensive gesture on the part of an advertising industry under increasingly severe attack in that period for putting direct commercial profits above broader social and environmental consideration: mere window dressing to ward off undesirable reactions from increasingly vocal consumer organisations or protective legislation from governments. Alternatively, and more relevant to this argument, it can be seen as a logical commercial reaction of firms preserving larger aggregate profits over the longer term at the cost of immediate returns. The motives are not important in this context but the consequent need to broaden the idea of marketing to include the deliberate influencing of the behaviour of targeted groups other than their direct purchasing behaviour opened up a whole new field. If people were to be encouraged to 'save energy', 'drive carefully' or 'take their litter home', then marketing was 'seeking to increase the acceptability of a social idea' (Kotler, 1986, p.193): it had become what is better termed *attitudinal marketing* as its intention was to alter or reinforce a set of attitudes held by targeted individuals. A number of aspects of this idea become clearly relevant to place marketing, offering the prospect of solutions to the problems raised earlier.

This sort of attitudinal marketing frequently involved the pursuit of social objectives which were frequently difficult to define with precision but often merged imperceptibly with the collective interest of society more usually assumed as a responsibility of public authorities. The concern with the longer- rather than the shorter-term profit led to the acceptance of a redefinition of the term 'profit' to include less easily measurable and more indirect social benefits. The attempts to influence behaviour beyond immediate purchasing activities provided scope for public authority campaigns. This had an important demonstration effect as much of this sort of marketing was conducted by, or on behalf of, public authorities, thus illustrating by example to those in public service the efficacy of marketing in general and familiarising them with its techniques. The demonstration of these possibilities together with the development of sets of techniques to operationalise them removed many of the objections that would otherwise have confronted place marketing.

*Image marketing*   To many practitioners of marketing it would seem superfluous to single out *image marketing* as a separate concept, for it is a truism that almost all goods and services are marketed to a greater or lesser degree through the promotion of images held by the consumer about them. It became increasingly apparent, however, in the course of the 1970s that images could be marketed while the product to which they are related remained only vaguely delineated in the background. For example, a new branch of marketing came into existence and was brought to technical perfection in the United States in the 1960s, to promote the images of politicians with little reference to policies. The growth of 'hearts and minds' campaigns for all sorts of objectives, not only once again demonstrated aspects of marketing, frequently in this case public relations operations, to public sector organisations, but also showed how the existence of a diffuse, complex and vaguely-defined product did not rule out the application of marketing techniques. The goal of image marketing is the manipulation of the behavioural patterns of selected audiences. Buying products (whether office space, houses, or shop goods), selecting entertainment, joining organisations, voting for a candidate or fighting for a cause, and many other forms of action responses are sought from people who are addressed by promotional activities. Obviously, places could be marketed through their generalised images even though the goods and services being sold were difficult to specify.

### An integrated concept of place marketing

Many of the ideas outlined above had in fact been for long a part of marketing practice; their elevation to the status of defined and discussed concepts, however, is a product of the last 15 years or so and is explainable in terms of the growth of marketing science as an organised study. They have emerged individually at different times in response to different situations, but taken together they can be used to underpin an integrated concept of place marketing, with its various spatial scale variants of national, regional or city marketing. They meet most of the objections raised earlier and thus provide both a logical justification and a guide to the selection of suitable techniques and procedures.

## Disciplinary contributions to place marketing

There is an obvious relationship between place marketing and economic theory. However, Fines (1981) recognises a contradiction between economics and marketing as the former relies on the basic assumption of 'economic man' as a rational, omniscient decision-maker while the latter conceives of 'the consumer' as an irrational persuadable deviation from the model. Such a distinction between these two assumptions was perhaps understandable given the characteristics of places as commodities and the assumed basis of much of traditional micro-economic theorising. As Stabler (1988) has argued, in an attempt to relate economic theory quite specifically with place promotion, conventional price theory cannot handle the multiple commodities that comprise the package on offer, and trade theory assumes a factor immobility; neither in addition find it easy to deal with non-priced resources.

However, the recognition that many goods and services have precisely these characteristics has encouraged a reformulation of economic approaches to accommodate them. In particular the attempts of economists to modify existing modelling techniques to enable such services as housing, with its substantial element of public provision, or recreation and tourism, where the product is a package of diverse elements to be approached analytically, is clearly relevant here. Similarly the relatively recent creation of the whole field of environmental economics offers a parallel development to the application of marketing to geographical areas.

Much of this reformulation refers back to Lancaster's (1966) recognition that commodities are not the object of the consumer search for utility as such but are purchased for the sake of certain of their characteristics or attributes. He further argued that, to use his terminology, commodities combine to generate activities which in turn combine to generate attitudes. The appropriateness of this line of thought to places as commodities is obvious but the problem lay in the application of analytical models capable of embracing such multifaceted commodities. Rugg (1971) attempted to apply Lancaster's ideas to tourism but excluded what he termed 'the geographical factors' which are generally precisely the attibutes of place of interest here. Far more relevant was the development by Brown *et al.* (1978) of the idea of *hedonic pricing*, that is, 'the implied or shadow price of a characteristic of a commodity'. This approach enabled non–traded commodities in the public sector such as housing or recreation services to be 'priced' and thus analysed as if in a commercial market situation.

Thus while marketing science with its focus on consumer behaviour was evolving sets of concepts applicable to the non–business sector, and was expanding its techniques to enable it to include products which were composed of many different elements, not all of which were priced, so also was economic science approaching much the same goals. The starting points, motivations and terminology were different but the result in both cases was that the attributes of places, previously dismissed as beyond the scope of analysis, could now become the object of analysis. Upon these theoretical and conceptual foundations a series of techniques and procedures could be constructed.

There is also a close relationship between place marketing and psychological theory. In particular marketing involves communication and especially the attempt to evoke a specific change in the attitude and thus behaviour of a *target group*. Communication theory has contributed studies of both the messages communicated and the behavioural responses (e.g. see Jowett and O'Donnell, 1986). Behaviour can be subdivided into two broad classes (cf. Triandis, 1977): *attributive* behaviour, that which is derived from the conclusions drawn about the internal states of others from observations of their behaviour; and *affective* behaviour, emotional reactions to people and events. An example of attributive behaviour would be a housing agency concluding that 'The occupancy rate of the dwellings in this neighbourhood is good, therefore they are very attractive'. Affective behaviour could be the experience of, for example, a burst of pride when the eye catches the Eiffel Tower in Paris, the Euromast in Rotterdam or the Statue of Liberty in New York. Similarly work on the strength and durability of behavioural patterns (Trandis, 1977) and the way repeated behaviour becomes habitual is of obvious relevance, because what is habitual is predictable and a 'script' for behaviour in similar future situations (Roloff and Miller, 1980). Psychological theory cannot other than underpin much of the discussion of promotion in Chapter 7.

The fundamental characteristic of cities is that they are places. This could be dismissed as a truism if it were not that the disciplines discussed so far, being intrinsically non-spatial, have usually failed to incorporate the spatial characteristics of places in their analysis, while conversely the science with a declared focus upon spatial characteristics, namely geography, has generally failed to incorporate a systematic analysis of markets within the study of places.

That is not to deny that the significance of the market to spatial activities has been recognised on various occasions in the geographical literature. In particular the considerable, possibly leading, contribution of geographical research to environmental cognition, will be evident in Chapters 6 and 7. The interest of geographers in the application of area-based public policies, mainly in cities, has been long and resulted in a voluminous literature about the spatial dimensions of urban problems and the spatial consequences of planning solutions. Many such contributions inevitably assess the efficacy of market-based approaches and agencies considered in Chapter 8. Similarly there was a stream of publications in the 1970s focusing on the functioning of various commercial markets in cities and the significance of the operation of these markets to urban development, such as the commercial office market (e.g. Bateman, 1986), or real estate and capital investment markets (e.g. Bourne, 1975, 1976). Davies (1976) even introduced the term 'marketing geography' to describe his research into retail distribution. These studies, however, confined their analysis to the spatial characteristics of the commercial sector of the economy, which was significantly often called the 'market sector'.

Although often making relevant contributions to important aspects, none of these attempt an analysis of the more comprehensive relationship between city and market implicit in our use of the term city marketing.

## City marketing and physical planning

The evolution of city marketing as an approach to planning in general was described in the previous chapter, where the idea of market planning emerged from other types of urban and regional planning. The role of city marketing within physical planning in particular can now be elaborated through a description of the distinctive characteristics of the city marketing plan itself.

A city marketing plan is inseparably linked with spatial policy, and especially with the physical structure plan which is largely instrumental in determining the dimensions of the future 'product'. The expectations and approaches of physical planning therefore form an important link between city marketing and spatial policy as a whole. As it now stands, there is an obvious difference in practice between the conventional urban planning approach and the city marketing planning approach. Physical planning is, at least in practice, to a considerable degree 'supply-oriented', i.e. the attention is usually focused on investigating the constraints and physical possibilities ('design') of the existing built environment. The 'demand'-side is often considered as a deduced phenomenon that is usually only treated in daily planning practice in terms of goals and objectives and seldom as an analytical subject to structure the treatment of the built environment. Marketing planning, however, is much more 'demand-oriented', i.e. the city and possible changes of the urban facility structure are considered from the perspective of the actual and potential consumers.

Conventional urban planning in the Netherlands was in practice strongly problem-oriented and prone to ad hoc reactions, not inaccurately described by Lindblom (1964) as 'muddling through'. Policy shifts were usually dictated by changes in what could be described as professional fashions and 'problem of the year' foci. Planning as an organisation has reacted 'bureaucratically', in the original Weberian sense of the word, that is the measures of success and the standards of practice were sought within the organisation, or more vaguely within the 'profession'. Over the last ten years, for example, a range of urban problems have been selected for intensive attention under such slogans as 'the urban manager', 'the compact city' and the rest which were not intended for consumption outside the town hall. Marketing planning on the other hand is far more

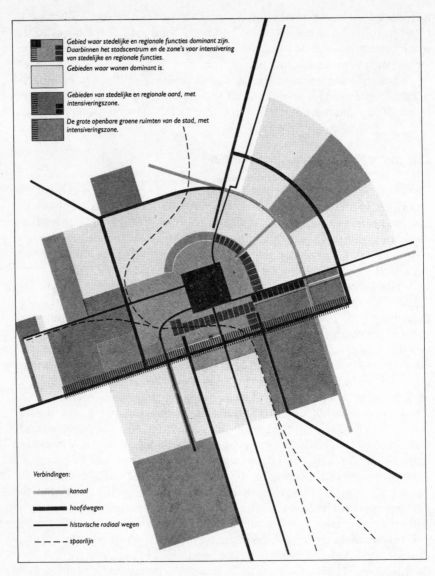

Gebied waar stedelijke en regionale functies dominant zijn.
Daarbinnen het stadscentrum en de zone's voor intensivering
van stedelijke en regionale functies.
Gebieden waar wonen dominant is.

Gebieden van stedelijke en regionale aard, met
intensiveringszone.

De grote openbare groene ruimten van de stad, met
intensiveringszone.

Verbindingen:

kanaal

hoofdwegen

historische radiaal wegen

spoorlijn

**Figure 2.1**  *Structure plan Groningen, 1986*

directly goal-oriented, linking the professionalism of the managers with the
users and potential users of the planned product. The 'interest groups' of
conventional planning are replaced by 'customers' which implies a different
relationship.

The establishment of a new framework for structure planning in the
Netherlands as a result of the 1985 Physical Planning Act (WRO/BRO 85)

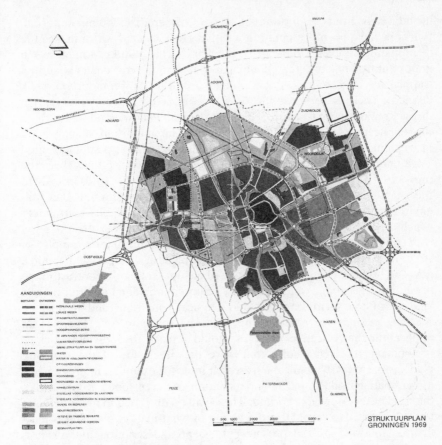

**Figure 2.2** *Structure plan Groningen, 1969*

provides an opportunity to examine the extent to which account has been taken of the new approach discussed above and of the new functions expected of physical planning. In comparison with the legislation governing planning before 1985 the new Act makes fewer demands on the structure plan as such and requires only 'a description in main lines of the future physical structure envisaged for the relevant area and its relations to neighbouring areas, together with an indication of the development phases anticipated'. The previously demanded statements of long-term policy have been replaced by an accent on the current situation of the planned area in relation to its immediate surroundings. There is thus an implicit invitation to produce relatively short-term policies, which could include urban marketing plans, for managing the spatial structure. A good example of a first step in this new direction is the structure plan for the city of Groningen from 1986 (see Figure 2.1).

Compared to its predecessor of 1969 (see Figure 2.2) the new plan, including its brief description, is much coarser. The dominant urban functions have been presented in a rather abstract way, which makes the resulting map appear almost to be the work of the painter Mondrian. An important task in marketing planning is to inform the consumers about the 'supply-side' and to invite them to make use of it (i.e. promotion broadly defined). There are other subtle differences of accent that together mark a distinct break with past approaches and implicitly allow, if not encourage, the application of marketing techniques. The important management instrument for the control of functional land-use change is supplemented by a more positive encouragement of the desirable rather than the prevention of the undesirable. The pursuit of such policies leads directly to the shaping and projection of suitable urban images through the built environment and similarly the removal of aspects of the built environment which contribute towards negative images of the city. In this way conventional urban spatial management by its control, for example, of street furniture, landscaping and even building design is operating within a new and broader management context of city marketing. In contrast to the preceding legislation, which explicitly required a detailed description and analysis of the socio-economic and physical conditions and trends, no specific demands for research are made by the new Act. There is an implication that selective research should replace the previous copious preliminary research studies that were the precursors of the structure plans. More directly applicable research into, for example, improvements in the 'spatial product' and an understanding of the customer groups within the market, are now appropriate. These will be discussed in more detail in later chapters. However, this discussion of what market planning is must first be followed by the prosaic but essential description of how it is performed.

# 3 City marketing as a planning tool

The previous chapter considered changes in the philosophy, objectives and methods of urban planning and in particular the growth of interest in what we have defined as market planning, i.e. the application of marketing approaches within public sector planning. Essentially, market planning involves procedures and strategies through which urban space is adapted as far as possible to accord with the wishes of selected target groups with the objective of creating the conditions for the efficient operation of the social and economic functions and activities of the area concerned. Such market planning when applied specifically in place management becomes geographical or place marketing and specifically in urban situations, city marketing. The purpose of this chapter is to treat this city marketing as a technique of planning, or more accurately a planning process incorporating a number of techniques. The central question will be 'how can city marketing be applied in practice within public sector planning?'

## The city marketing process

Urban market planning in some form has long been accepted as being essential in preventing market failures. Evidently, an inefficiently operating housing, education or health service market will have a direct negative effect on the total urban production system. An oversupply of such facilities in relation to demand is clearly wasteful of scarce public resources and may even be damaging to other attributes such as environmental amenity, while an undersupply of such facilities as housing, schools, publically provided health or recreation facilities is at the very least a disincentive to new exogenous investment or residents.

In general, there are several types of planning intervention by central or local governments in case of market failure which have long been practised in many countries. These include:

1.  the provision of information about an area as a whole to encourage desirable private developments if these are retarded through the lack of such information;

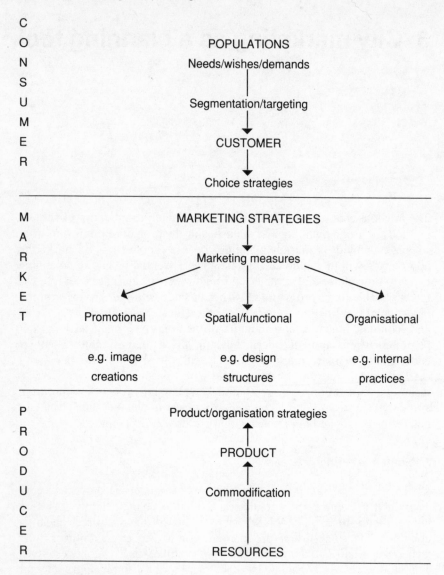

**Figure 3.1**   *Main elements in a city marketing process*

2.  the provision of a stimulus through the improvement of publically provided economic or environmental infrastructure;
3.  the provision of direct or indirect financial subsidies to make the balance of costs and benefits more attractive;
4.  the regulation of development in the market to prevent urban functions becoming self-defeating by damaging the resources on which they thrive.

The main lines of city marketing as a procedure are relatively easy to describe, although less easy to operationalise (see also Ashworth and Voogd, 1987). The main elements contained in any marketing process can be summarised as in Figure 3.1, whereby ultimately populations and resources are brought together so that the needs of the former are satisfied by the products derived from the latter. This conjunction is achieved within the market by means of various sorts of marketing measures. Each of these elements will be discussed at length later in the context of city marketing as a specialised form of the general marketing process.

The translation of this ordered array of elements into a workable operational tool of city planning involves its reformulation in a number of ways. In summary, such a procedure consists of the manipulation of four basic elements, namely:

1.  the analysis of the market, or more usually markets;
2.  the delineation of the city or region as place-product;
3.  the establishment of the goals of the exercise and therefore type of strategic policy;
4.  the determination of the policy instruments or 'marketing mix', and their elaboration in the light of the strategy mentioned above in more operational terms.

Consequently, a city marketing process usually will proceed along the general lines of Figure 3.2. In order to appreciate the deeper implications of this conceptual scheme, a number of more general comments should be made here.

Both this and the preceding figure, however, as they are arranged, suffer from what might be termed the determinism of the printed page, as the tendency to read from top to bottom in one continuous sequence is almost unavoidable. It should be clearly stated at the outset that this and most of the subsequent phase diagrams in this chapter are not simple 'critical path' procedures for three obvious but important reasons. First, it is possible, although whether desirable or not will be argued later, to order the phases in a wide variety of ways. Secondly, progress through the successive action phases will allow, and even encourage changes in preceding phases, which are therefore logically never completed as they are continuously subject to adjustment as a result of information feedback. Thirdly, and this will be stressed at length later, the process is reiterative, that is its full cycle is repeated continuously until its objectives are perceived to have been attained.

The first phase is the market reconnaissance in which the existing consumer markets and the existing urban and/or regional facility structure are examined with the objective of determining which marketing strategy is appropriate. The functions of the city or region, or the city or region as a whole, must be *commodified*, that is treated as a product or set of products

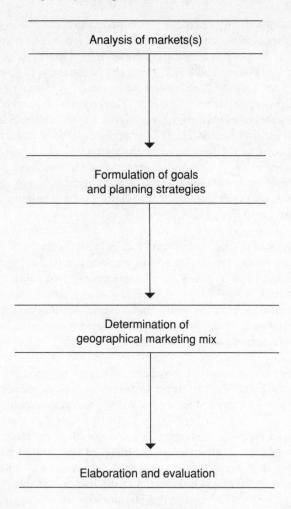

Figure 3.2    *Major phases of a city marketing process*

which must be *positioned*, that is viewed in terms of its competitive position, actually or potentially, in relation to other products and yet whose characteristics are in practice far more difficult to define than most commercially traded goods and services. Similarly the actual or potential users of such a product must be viewed in terms of targeted market segments. The linkage between product and consumer is a multifaceted relationship examined through the *auditing* of the producers, in this case the public agencies. This will be discussed in more detail in a later section.

Despite what was implied in some of the early literature on this topic there is no single possible correct marketing strategy open to urban public authorities, and an important task is to decide what sort of marketing is appropriate for a particular set of functions in a particular place. Various policy goals can be pursued which might be *conservational*, the maintenance of current levels of service, *stimulational*, the shaping of conditions that encourage new activities, *integrational* or many others. It is likely that the goals of public policy will be both more varied, more long term and less amenable to quantification, than those of commercial organisations. Although this does not prevent the application of marketing techniques, it does render the prior establishment of explicit policy strategies, objectives and priorities more important.

After the formulation of the goals and policy strategies, the *marketing mix* must be determined. This is a phrase developed as long ago as the 1920s (Jefferson and Lickorish, 1988) to describe the combination of measures needed to achieve the desired strategy. After discussions lasting many years there is now general agreement that it is impossible to determine an exact optimal marketing mix, if only because the various elements in it are themselves interrelated so that success or otherwise as a result of the application of one set of measures itself alters the input need from others and thus the balance of the entire mix. In practice the marketing mix needs constant monitoring as to its effects upon the market and thus constant adjustment of the elements within it. In contrast to the marketing mix usually found in traditional business applications, a *geographical marketing mix* may be defined as a combination of at least the following sets of instruments:

1. promotional measures;
2. spatial-functional measures;
3. organisational measures;
4. and, last but of considerable importance, financial measures.

The scope and effectiveness of city and regional marketing policies will be largely determined by the selection and application of the appropriate combination of these measures. This selection, together with statements concerning the goals and objectives to be pursued can form the basis of an urban (or regional) marketing plan. The idea of instrument combination needs to be stressed, given the tendency, exemplified later, of promotion alone being implemented as a surrogate for the entire marketing system outlined here. In addition the implementation of any one of the sets of measures is likely to have implications for the effectiveness of the others. For example, measures operating in spatial design features will contribute towards urban images and thus reinforce, or contradict, promotional measures. Therefore, integration as well as combination should be guiding principles. This point will be further discussed and applied to particular case studies later.

The above mentioned marketing mix instruments usually require a phased implementation, which necessitates simultaneously both the evaluation of their effectiveness and efficiency and the elaboration or refinement of the chosen planning strategies. This will be illustrated later by means of some actual market planning processes in the Netherlands.

## Analysis of the markets

An important activity in any geographical marketing process is market analysis. This concerns the study of both the spatial and organisational structure of the city or region as product ('the supply side') as well as the characteristics, market behaviour and needs of the identified users as consumers ('the demand side'). The identification of both supply and demand can provide some difficulties, as will be described in the following two chapters. In comparison with many commercial products, marketing a geographical entity like a city may be the sale of both a related package of urban functions, and in some cases the sale of the idea of the city as a whole. Not only is this product necessarily diffuse, difficult to identify and even to delimit in spatial terms but it is also distinctive in a number of ways (see Ashworth and de Haan, 1986). This distinction stems in part from the nature of publicly traded goods as opposed to commercial products and in part from the intrinsic characteristics of places. The attributes of the product which derive from these characteristics will be considered at length in Chapter 5, but it can be noted here that the analysis of place markets is as a result necessarily both different and usually more complex than described in most such marketing exercises designed for commercial products.

Similarly on the demand side most urban studies divide populations into categories according to single demographic, social or functional character-istics, which are not particularly relevant to market analysis where it is the consumption behaviour specifically that is important. Consumers, or potential consumers, generally have more than one motive and engage in more than one activity as 'users' of urban facilities, and their consumption behaviour can only be determined in relation to their use of a particular aspect of the city. This implies that a much more flexible approach to the urban consumer market is required than is achieved by the use of the traditional socio-economic classifications that are widely used in urban social geography, as will be elaborated in Chapter 4.

The effectiveness of the city, its organisation and its working methods, in meeting the requirements of the market is assessed through so-called *auditing*. These are analytical exercises designed to obtain an impression of the various qualities of the urban product in relation to its market. Auditing results in a better insight into the possible targets and measures to be taken. This will be examined at length in the next chapter.

On the basis of the information collected on the characteristics of the product (in this case the city, region or aspects of them) and the consumer

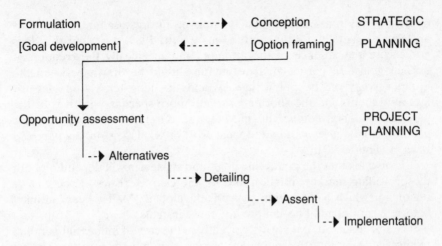

**Figure 3.3**   *A strategic planning network for non-profit organisations* (after Nott, 1984)

(the user of the urban or regional facilities) a series of choices can be made in the policy determination phase. These include the choice of targeted consumer groups on the demand side and the current appropriateness of the facilities and need for change, what has been called *product positioning* in the market (e.g. see Gwinner *et al.*, 1977).

## Marketing goals and strategies

The determination of marketing goals, and strategies for attaining them, are likely to be more important in public planning than in the private sector, as well as being more difficult to determine and demanding more attention within the marketing process. Although commercial organisations may have a wide variety of stated or assumed objectives, some of which are similar to those of public authorities such as local identification, social and community responsibilities (topics discussed at length in Chapter 8) and the like, the principal dominant, and at least in the long term survival determining objective, must be the relatively simple one of profit making. Public authorities on the other hand have a much more complex task in assessing, balancing and ordering collective benefits, and thereby establishing the goals of the marketing operation. Even when the policies of private and public organisations are very similar, the objectives that motivate them are likely to be very different (see Capon, 1981, for a further analysis and illustration of this point).

Strategy determination, as practised in many private organisations, may be 'less useful in a service producing non–profit organisation, where aims are always vague and often contentious' (Nott, 1984, p.57) but this does not excuse the absence of the attempt, and specifically the creation of explicit goals. In particular a distinction should be drawn between the broader goals of the public agency and the long–term strategies for attaining them, and the shorter-term and more specific objectives of the particular intervention in the market: the difference between *strategic planning goal determination* and what Nott (1984) labels *project planning strategy* (Figure 3.3).

It is obvious that the marketing goals and strategies will depend on both the prevailing market situation and on the characteristics of the city or region for which a marketing policy is developed. As has been outlined before, a careful auditing can provide these insights.

It can be assumed, not always correctly in the case of influential national public agencies, that the individual organisation must accept the general market situation as given. For example, it has been suggested by Eldridge (1971) that the three most commonly encountered overall market conditions (listed in Table 3.1) should be met by three different, equally general, strategy responses. Much more flexibility, however, is possible when considering the appropriate strategic response to the wide range of possible organisational goals, themselves determined by the nature of the city. Table 3.2 shows one typology of marketing types based on the targeted market and upon the urban structure in which four possible types of policy can be distinguished.

**Table 3.1**  Market situation and strategic choice (after Eldridge, 1971)

| Market situation | Appropriate strategy |
| --- | --- |
| Buyers' market | Maximise customer satisfaction |
| Sellers' market | Maximise production |
| Low activity market | Conserve resources |

**Table 3.2**  A typology of types of city marketing policy

| Market | Urban facility structure | |
| --- | --- | --- |
| Adapt | Maintain | |
| Existing consumers | 1. Consolidation | 2. Quality |
| New consumers | 3. Expansion | 4. Diversification |

A consolidation or defensive policy (option 1) is needed when it is desirable to maintain the existing structure of urban services for the existing consumer groups. This is an appropriate strategy for cities which have no particular spatial socio-economic problems presently or in the foreseeable future. Their only problem is that 'competing' cities may become more attractive in the near future, thus threatening a reallocation of investments and/or purchasing power. A quality–oriented policy (option 2) will concentrate upon providing better facilities for the same consumers. This option is appropriate, for example, for cities with an obsolete or inefficient functional and/or physical structure. An expansion policy (option 3) will seek out new markets for the existing urban services. This policy is clearly relevant in cities with latent resources as yet relatively undeveloped. For example a town with many potentially exploitable old buildings, but with only a modest number of heritage tourists, could reasonably pursue a marketing strategy directed towards promoting the urban 'cultural heritage' to this market.

Finally, a diversification policy (option 4) will seek out new targeted markets for a new set of services. No doubt this is the most ambitious city marketing strategy, because it implies both an adaptation of the urban facility structure and a thorough marketing campaign to attract new users for these facilities. An example could be a city with a very small share of households with above-average incomes, which aims at attracting this target group through a specific housing and cultural 'revitalisation' programme.

It has been argued (van der Veen and Voogd, 1987) from empirical experience that public bodies, and in particular local authorities, have indulged in either what could be termed *minimal marketing*, i.e. a belief that the product more or less sells itself without ostensible promotion, or conversely *aggressive marketing*, where the realisation that an existing product, the result perhaps of previous over-investment without regard to the market situation, must be sold to a wider public if its survival is to be ensured. The former is often little more than a justification for complacency and the latter is an example of a product rather than market orientation.

It is theoretically conceivable that *non-marketing* is an appropriate response. Such a situation could occur where the urban product is so incapable of satisfying a consumer demand attracted to it that it is better if attention is not drawn to it (on the principle of the adage, 'the best way to kill-off a poor product is to advertise it'). This could only be regarded as a temporary expedient, appropriate during the period while active product improvement (e.g. urban renovation policies) was being undertaken and thus better labelled *non-premature marketing*. In contrast to these extremes there is frequently a case to be made for what can be termed *balanced marketing*, in which the short-term satisfaction of the consumer and the longer-term goals of the authority, which in turn presumably encompass the less immediate welfare of consumers as a whole, are both included as objectives of the marketing strategy and balanced through marketing measures.

## Marketing measures

Physical marketing plans generally aim at some combination of three objectives as part of these wider strategies, namely:

1.  *developmental* objectives, which provide a stimulus for new activities;
2.  *organisational* efficiency objectives, which provide a framework for the integration of different urban policies with spatial consequences;
3.  *promotional* objectives, which supply selected information about the city's potential products to potential users of them.

In order to meet these objectives, marketing measures must be used, as is illustrated in Figure 3.1. These marketing measures may be promotional measures, such as the creation of images aimed at creating or reinforcing desirable consumer behaviour; spatial-functional measures, such as elements of the physical design; organisational measures, improving the operation of the authority as a result of the auditing exercises mentioned earlier and described in more detail in the next chapter; or any combination of these and more. It is important to note that the implementation of any one of these set of measures is likely to affect the others, so that in practice an integrated approach utilising a selected combination of these actions is generally the most effective.

Marketing measures attempt to evoke a specific change in the attitude and thus consequently behaviour of clients. This may be done directly, through promotion, but also indirectly through other measures such as organisational or spatial–functional measures. The change sought is a specific response from a targeted group. Persuasion theory suggests that there are three different forms of response possible from such 'audiences' (see Roloff and Miller, 1980).

First, marketing measures may be *response shaping*. This is similar to learning, in which the information source (e.g. new street furniture, promotion brochure, advertisement, etc.) is a teaching device and the target person or potential customer a pupil. Promotional activities may attempt to shape the response of a target group by 'teaching' it how to behave and offer positive reinforcement to learning. For example, 'see our new pedestrian area and enjoy your shopping!'. If group responses favourable to the urban manager's purpose are reinforced by rewards to the audience, positive attitudes are developed towards what is learned. In this kind of response to marketing measures, the target group satisfies a need for positive reinforcement, and the manager satisfies a need for a desired response from the target group.

Secondly, measures may be *response reinforcing*. If the target population already has positive attitudes towards an urban product, whether specific or general, the urban manager reminds them about the positive aspects of the image and encourages them to demonstrate their attitudes through specific forms of behaviour. As we will illustrate in the next sections, many public planning activities in today's urban society are response reinforcing (fund raising, seeking political support, investments, and so on).

Thirdly, marketing measures may be *response changing*. This is the most difficult task because it involves asking people to switch from one perceived image to another, from one attitude to another, to change behaviour, or to adopt new behaviour. People are reluctant to change; thus, in order to convince them to do so, the urban manager has to relate the change to something in which the target person already believes. In persuasion theory this is called an 'anchor' (Roloff and Miller, 1980), because it is already accepted by the target person and will be used to tie down new attitudes or behaviour. An anchor, which may be an existing belief, value or group norm, is a starting point for change because it represents something that is already widely accepted by the potential customers of the city.

## Marketing planning as an iterative process

In city marketing planning practice an iterative process is usually followed to implement the measures described above (Voogd, 1987a, 1988). The general characteristics of such a 'cyclical process' are shown in Figure 3.4.

An essential characteristic of this iterative process is that after each iteration the various steps will be more detailed, and more operational. Step 1 is called the 'search for direction'. In the first round this may be the launching of an idea, in the following rounds this may involve more complex tasks such as an extensive 'auditing' to analyse the strengths, weaknesses, opportunities and problems of the organisation in relating market to product. Step 1 results in a 'plan' (step 2).

The notion 'plan' must be broadly interpreted, for instance in the first iteration ('launching idea') the entire 'plan' may be written on one single sheet of paper, announcing the intention to write a report, structure scheme or project plan on a designated issue in following rounds. The activities in step 3 are all directed to winning support for the plan developed in step 2. If there is not enough evident support alternative directions need to be considered, which may imply that the whole process returns to step 1.

Step 3 is, to a large extent, devoted to information and communication activities. There is of course a strong relationship with the way the 'plan' of step 2 is presented, because at this point McCluhan's famous dictum 'The Medium is the Message' has particular significance. The promotional

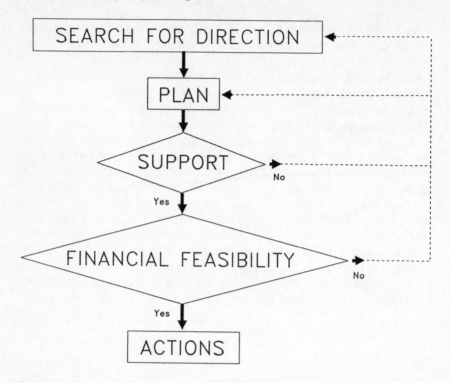

**Figure 3.4**  *Incentive-orientated market planning as an iterative process*

function of the plans implies that considerable attention is devoted to its design and layout.

Step 4, the financial-economic feasibility or implementation of the proposals, will not be emphasised in each round. However, the more iterations there have been, the more important this step will become. It often also includes the investigation of organisational constructions, such as various forms of partnership with other public or private agencies.

Finally, step 5 in this market planning process can be labelled 'actions'. In the first round this may mean that organisational and budgetary measures are taken to support plan-making and research in the next iteration. In following rounds this step may involve the start of implementation planning or even the start of actual physical building activities.

The structure of the market planning process of Table 3.3 can be recognised in several Dutch urban revitalisation programmes (as described in more detail later in this chapter). An important characteristic of this process is that each round or iteration results in a 'refinement', for instance in the case of step 2:

1.  from idea to proposal;
2.  from proposal to formal plan;

3. from formal plan to proposal for elaboration areas;
4. from elaboration proposal to elaboration plan;
5. from elaboration plan to inter-agency agreements, etc.

**Table 3.3** A plan-making approach for a market-oriented structure plan

| Planning phase | Objective |
| --- | --- |
| inventory and analysis of threats and possibilities | External audit |
| inventory and analysis of strengths and weaknesses | Internal audit |
| determination of target groups and submarket concerned | Definition of demand side |
| analysis of opinions target groups with regard to the various submarkets | Interferences between demand and supply |
| formulation of possible adaptations supply-side and elaboration areas | Definition of supply side |
| public discussions about draft structure plan | Start promotion |
| definitive structure plan formulating teams for elaboration areas | Invitation to private investments |
| start planmaking elaboration areas | Establishment of public-private partnerships |

This process also differs from conventional planning schemes in the intentions of step 5. The 'actions' in the various rounds are mainly directed *to enabling the next iteration to occur*. It is evident that this in turn affects the content of the plan (step 2), which must offer enough points of contact for further attention, for instance by designating 'elaboration areas', i.e. areas for which additional plan–making should take place, or by offering financial or other incentives.

## Some illustrative cases

In order to illustrate an application of the market planning approach outlined in Figure 3.5, two cases will be examined. The first at the scale of the individual town, which has little control over the external market factors and is thus basically reactive to its situation, and secondly an attempt at the national scale to redefine the role of cities within markets where some influence upon the external environments can be exercised.

The first, a planning study based on this procedure and designed to arrive at a structure plan for the Dutch town of Hoogeveen, will be briefly discussed (see Pellenbarg *et al.*, 1988). The town is situated at the 'front door' of the three northern provinces of the Netherlands. It has a population of approximately 50,000 inhabitants and performs various commercial and social services for the southern part of the province of Drenthe.

Compared to the scheme given in Figure 3.2, a more detailed procedure has been followed, but the intentional steps can still be clearly recognised.

The process began with an inventory and analysis of the problems and possibilities of the town. Important issues in this phase were, amongst others, the enlargement in scale of many socio-economic activities and the impacts of recent developments in technology. In addition, a first analysis of the strengths and weaknesses of Hoogeveen was made, in which almost every significant function of the town was evaluated. Next, the target groups were defined. Each urban function (shopping areas, offices, recreation areas, etc.) was related to a particular submarket, by means of an analytical framework which included actual and potential users (an approach elaborated in Chapter 4).

The next phase was to analyse the reactions and opinions of the various target groups with respect to the town's different functions. Several techniques have been used to cover the various groups, such as street interviews, telephone enquiries and questionnaires. The resulting information was used to elaborate the strengths and weaknesses, defined earlier in the internal audit, and to formulate for each neighbourhood a shortlist of possible improvements and alterations from the 'client's' point of view. In addition, a more balanced attempt was made to arrive at a draft structure plan. Very important elements of this plan are the so-called elaboration areas, which may be spatially or functionally defined, or more usually combinations of both. These are specific areas that are worthwhile elaborating for reasons of complexity and/or market appeal in a later stage. Such elaboration exercises may be conducted together with representatives of selected target groups, so that various forms of 'partnership' developments may be arrived at. The draft structure plan is used as an instrument to stimulate public discussion among current users of the town and to inform other government bodies and potential users about the potentials and priorities under consideration in the town.

An example of such an exercise is *competition analysis* which can be operationalised for any group of functions (Bouwers and Pellenbarg, 1989). The competitive situation of a city as viewed from the enterprise is compared with the actual situation existing in the town. The features selected for consideration and the weightings assigned to them, are derived from the 'enterprise climate', i.e. the perceived competitive situation for a particular activity. This approach will be outlined in more detail in Chapter 4.

The structure of the market planning process, as outlined in Figure 3.5, can also be recognised at the national scale, in the recent 'Fourth Report on Physical Planning' of the Dutch government (1988). This, and each of the three preceding reports since the Second World War (1960, 1966, 1975), can be seen as both a reflection of the prevailing conventional wisdom in planning and a set of guidelines for the more detailed subsequent provincial, regional and local plans. The fourth such national report is in marked contrast to those immediately preceding it in its broad brush approach, and its switch of emphasis from the amelioration of the consequences of economic growth, such as congestion, environmental damage and regional inequalities, to an attention upon encouraging the conditions within which further growth will occur. Earlier 'iterations' in this market planning process of the fourth report consisted of the widespread publication of a report on infrastructure policy (RPD, 1986) and a report on 'spatial perspectives' (RPD, 1987). Both reports were used by the national planners to organise informal meetings around the country to raise the level of anticipation for the coming 'official' governmental fourth report. In this report several policy actions were announced with the intention of stimulating or supporting further initiatives of provincial and local governments.

The city of Groningen, for example, is seen in the fourth national report as the northern centre of economic activity. It is seen as functioning as both an outlier of the main national cockpit of economic activity in the Western Netherlands and also expected to act as the generator of economic expansion for the rest of the northern region. The planning task in the light of these assumptions is clearly to facilitate development by a combination of judicious public infrastructural investment and the engendering and promotion of a suitable climate for new and existing private economic activities (Voogd, 1987a; Raggers and Voogd, 1989). Groningen's structure plan for the main lines of development of the city itself can be regarded as a more detailed implementation of the general ideas of the national plan (see Figure 2.1). In particular a clear choice has been made for a stimulational rather than a regulatory tone to the policies proposed. Two main objectives are stressed, first the strengthening of the so-called central functions of the city in relation to its region and secondly the improvement in the residential enironment of the city's inhabitants. The ordering is in itself interesting, being a reversal of previous priorities, and in practice the second objective has been relegated to subsequent lower level district plans.

The main instrument for the attainment of these goals is the development of key selected sites which are intended to provide an example and a symbolic public commitment to a climate of enterprise that will encourage private participation: a clear example of what Nelissen (1989) has called the 'Grandes Projets' technique. In other words, in this urban structure plan, as in the national fourth report, use is again made of the instrument of 'elaboration areas' to stimulate discussions and thus private initiatives in certain areas. The shift from *regulatory planning* to what is called *incentive planning* is illustrated by the attention paid to these 'show' sites. An example is the 'Verbindingskanaal Zone': an area alongside a canal just to the south of the inner city around the existing main railway station and main access route to the city centre (see Figure 3.5). As part of an elaboration of the structure plan, an urban design process has been started under the supervision of a few highly paid consultant architects. The resulting plan includes, among other things, architectural designs for new office development around the station, and new transport interchange facilities. The various architectural designs provoked considerable and vociferous public discussion, especially on the controversial new high-rise apartment complex on an artificial island in the middle of the southern ring canal. This was intended to provide high amenity accommodation for high income small households who might be tempted to come 'back to the city' and was a highly visible and provocative symbol. Clearly success was achieved in the intention of stimulating the interest of both local citizens and private investors, stimulating the production of ideas and generally focusing public attention. The debate itself was used as a necessary preliminary to the emergence of new partnership arrangements and working methods useful in the revitalisation of this part, and by extension other areas, of Groningen (Raggers, 1989).

## Procedure or philosophy?

The problems facing urban planning and the constraints under which planning authorities operate produced the imperatives described in Chapter 1. The concepts discussed in Chapter 2 provide the logical basis upon which the procedures discussed in this chapter can be constructed. However, this description of how market planning can be conducted, and the elaboration of the most important components which will form the content of later chapters, must be constantly related to the wider context of public sector urban planning.

**Figure 3.5**   *Groningen: plan for an elaboration area (near Central Station)*

The initial question implicitly posed but not directly answered in this chapter is whether market planning is a specific procedure, one of many instruments available to the urban planner, to be applied in appropriate situations, or, alternatively, is it a pervading philosophy of planning, a way of identifying, defining and solving urban problems, in brief a distinctive way of managing cities? There are reasons to advocate the latter. Many of the methods and procedures of market planning are already very familiar. For instance, the iterative process of Figure 3.4 bears a resemblance to other 'cyclic planning' concepts, for instance those suggested by McLoughlin (1969) or the 'strategic choice approach' (e.g. see Friend and Jessop, 1969; Hickling, 1974). However, the central themes in a market planning process are not 'choices' or 'uncertainty'. The central theme of market planning can be denoted as *'will-shaping'*, i.e. the forming of a common mental faculty by which people deliberately choose to decide upon a course of action. In this respect market planning is clearly being used in the illustrations as part of a 'communication structure' as developed by such planning theorists as Habermas (1973) or van Gunsteren (1976). Such themes will be raised again later in relation to other cases, but first the three components of the marketing process, the market, the product and the measures must be considered in more detail.

# 4 Analysing the market

An effective city marketing approach always necessitates the study of both the spatial and organisational structure of the city as product as well as the characteristics, market behaviour and needs of the identified users as consumers. 'On the basis of the information collected on the characteristics of the city, or aspects of it, and the user of the city's facilities, a series of choices can be made in the policy determination phase. These include the choice of targeted consumer groups on the demand side and the current appropriateness of the urban product to such groups, and consequent possible need for adaptation, on the supply side. In marketing terms this process is known as *product positioning* (described in more detail in, for example, Gwinner *et al.*, 1977). This will be discussed in the next sections.

## Auditing the market

It is not unusual for local politicians or officers to welcome marketing as a means of promoting what amounts to little more than their wishful thinking about the city to a wider audience. One of the first things they have in mind is to prepare some 'flashy' colourful brochures, containing vague but far–reaching intentions, thus hoping to project a progressive and 'in touch' image to their voters. Often, however, this image betrays only a lack of knowledge of the reality of the city upon which such policies are based. The effectiveness of city marketing depends to a large extent on the quality of its preparation, including particularly the thoroughness of the research activities that support it. An essential phase therefore, as mentioned in the preceding chapter, is that of 'auditing'. Auditing implies a systematic analysis of the market position of a city in relation to both the external environment (i.e. its competitive context within wider national and inter-national developments) as well as that internal to the city itself (i.e. its physical, social, economic and organisational qualities).

A distinction can be made between an 'external audit' and an 'internal audit' (see Figure 4.1). An *external audit* concerns the analysis of issues which cannot be influenced to any realistic extent by the urban or regional

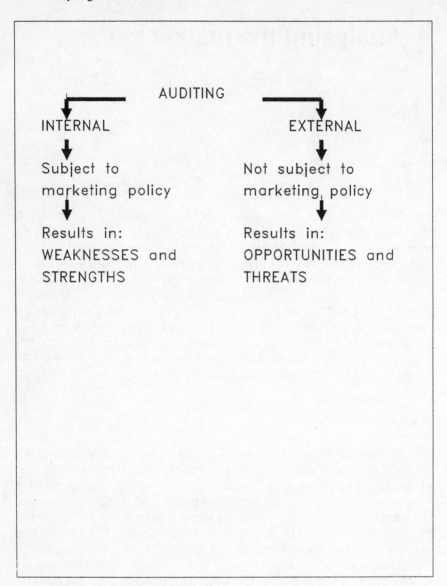

**Figure 4.1**   *Structure of audit phase*

authorities. Examples of these issues include national and international economic developments, changing consumer habits, technological developments, and so forth. Through this external audit the organisation will gain insight into the opportunities, problems or threats that surround it. The performance of the organisation can be compared with that of actual and potential competitors. An *internal audit* deals with issues that

can be influenced by the policy of the urban or regional authorities. The purpose of this kind of audit is to create an overview of the weaknesses and
strengths of the 'product' in terms of extrinsic rather than intrinsic qualities. Sometimes, the acronym SWOT or SWOP is used in marketing studies to show such strengths-weaknesses, and opportunities-threats/problems analyses of the organisation in relating market to product. Various methods which can be used to perform this will be discussed later in this chapter.

Auditing should result in sets of broad conclusions that form the basis for
future policy initiatives. The external audit especially provides evidence for the marketing strategies and goals, whereas the internal audit will give direction to policies for adapting the urban or regional product to meet the demands of future users.

Important questions to be answered by an external audit are:

1. What are the major developments in various economic sectors (e.g. industry, office and service sectors)?
2. What are the major social developments (e.g. household characteristics, life-style issues)?
3. What are the major relevant policies of other public authorities that bear upon these issues (e.g. authorities with responsibility for different levels in the jurisdictional hierarchy, such as regional, national or even supra-national bodies, and agencies with sectoral responsibilities, such
   as tourist boards, development authorities and the like)?
4. What are the major developments in, and policies of, other neighbouring and competing cities?

These questions can clearly be elaborated and analysed in various ways. One way is to use some kind of a 'brainstorm' method, bringing together in some structured sessions one or more groups of experts in various fields. Another way is by performing 'traditional' desk-research, perhaps supplemented by a number of interviews with selected experts. However, an external audit should at the end always result in a concise overview of the opportunities and threats faced by the city, preferably on one or two A4 sheets rather than buried in a 200–page report.

An internal audit will focus on the city and its organisation. Important questions are:

1. How do the users perceive the various urban products?
2. Which aspects of these products are highly appreciated and which are less appreciated?
3. Which aspects or products are felt to be missing in the city?

4. How effective and efficient were past policies in meeting user requirements?
5. How effective and efficient are current organisational structures in relating services to users?

These questions can also be elaborated and refined in various ways. The resulting answers should provide information about the strengths and weaknesses of the urban products, thus enabling planners and city managers to decide what further action should be taken. To perform a full internal audit, knowledge should be available about the various urban submarkets. Thus some kind of a market segmentation should be performed. This issue will be discussed in the next section. Later in this chapter we will return to the auditing activity by elaborating a complete research framework for city market analysis.

## Market segmentation

It has never been enough merely to acknowledge that public services exist within a market: that market must be targeted by means of *segmentation* into its relevant parts. The definition of the meaning of markets is clearly of importance in this context and deserves more attention than it has received. Most social science taxonomies are based on single variable demographic or functional characteristics, and result in such categories as shoppers, workers, tourists, residents and the like. These are both methodologically dubious (see Ashworth and de Haan, 1986) and not particularly relevant to market planning. The target groups generally have more than one motive and engage in more than one activity as users of urban facilities and their consumption behaviour can only be determined in relation to their use of a particular aspect of the city. This implies that a much more flexible approach to the urban consumer market is required than is achieved by the use of the traditional socio-economic classifications that are widely used in urban social geography.

Market segmentation has been defined as a 'process whereby management recognises the existence of different demand curves in the market and adapts the company's marketing strategy accordingly' (Davis, 1986, p.69). In other words, market segmentation implies the breaking down of a roughly defined mass market into segments or subgroups. This is not in itself new as trade will always imply some form of market segmentation (Young *et al.* 1978). But it is rarely practised to any degree in city marketing, which is particularly unfortunate as it provides urban managers with the background necessary to develop targeted marketing strategies and targeted campaigns. Using market segmentation analysis, city planners have the ability to shape an urban product to specific users and to target messages to specific audiences.

There are as many ways to segment a market as there are to slice a pie.

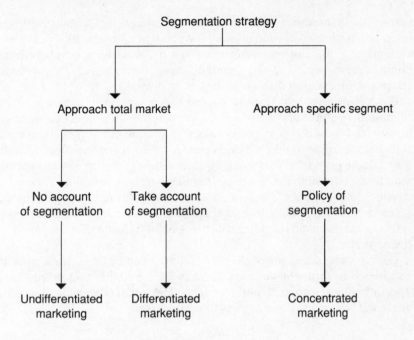

**Figure 4.2**   *Types of segmentation strategy*

The various segmentation options available are outlined in Figure 4.2. One of three different types of segmentation strategies can be selected: a concentrated strategy, focusing on only one segment within the population; a differentiated strategy, selecting several segments and developing tailored marketing plans for each; or an undifferentiated strategy, treating all consumers or users as similar and offering a standard approach for everyone.

The most basic forms of market segmentation are into users and non-users, first time and repeat purchasers, and early or late adopters of new products, each of which requires a quite different marketing strategy. Equally basic is the classification of users by the intensity of their use, with the well known 80/20 rule (i.e. 80 per cent of product consumption is derived from 20 per cent of customers), being applicable in several public services. These fundamental initial segmentation actions could, and would in most commercial companies, be dismissed as obvious but in fact are rarely performed for most local public services.

More sophisticated segmentation can be based upon demographic or spatial criteria, which are likely to be particularly relevant to local services supplied on criteria of need. Much commercial marketing is based upon so-called 'psychographic' variables derived from customers **AIO**s (i.e. Activities, Interests and Opinions). One of the problems of applying market segmentation is that its conceptual simplicity is matched by its operational complexity, and information about many of the above customer variables are difficult to collect, although it should be remembered that public sector organisations generally have better access to available statistical information than do most private firms.

Product-derived information, however, is more easily available to the organisation, thus allowing segmentation based upon product class, brand loyalty and product positioning. Finally, it is worth noting that much commercial segmentation is based upon so-called *buyer benefits*, that is the way a single product is purchased by quite different groups of consumers in search of quite different benefits. It is likely to be a revealing exercise to consider many public services in terms not of the product, whether recreation facility, public transport service, or environmental plan, but in terms of the quite different benefits being enjoyed by different segments of the market.

Once distinct segments of the market have been isolated, these must be considered in terms of their measurability, accessibility and profitability. The definition of these criteria is dependent, understandably, upon the goals and resources of the organisation concerned.

### Geographical behaviour as basis for segmentation

Segmentation based on geographical behaviour can be used to delineate groups who use an urban function and those who do not. It can also be used to segment a range of behaviour in the use of functions, such as frequency, purpose and timing. An approach that has been used to classify consumers or potential consumers according to their geographical behaviour is outlined below.

For every urban function (shopping areas, offices, recreation areas, etc.) related to a particular submarket, an analytical framework similar to Figure 4.3 was used to define actual and potential users. For example, a shopping area may be used by people living in the city (group I), but also by people from outside the city (group III). There may also be some people who do their shopping elsewhere, although they live in the city under consideration (group II). Finally, we have the 'rest of the world': people who do not live in the city analysed, nor use its functions (group IV). This framework can then be used to analyse the opinions of people belonging to the four segments using relevant information–gathering techniques. The resulting information can be used to define and elaborate the strengths and weaknesses for the internal audit, and to formulate for each urban neighbourhood a shortlist of possible improvements and alterations from the 'client's' point of view. Clearly, this provides very useful information to prepare target group oriented physical plans.

The operation of Figure 4.3 may be illustrated by the shopping function.

| | User of the function | Non-user of the function |
|---|:---:|:---:|
| residing | I | II |
| non-residing | III | IV |

**Figure 4.3**    *Framework to define and analyse target groups*

A shopping centre may be used both by people who live in the city (category I) as by people who live in the surrounding region (category III). It is relatively easy to collect information about these users, e.g. by street interviews in or near the shopping centre. This information may be familiar consumer identifiers, including demographic and geographical variables such as age, gender, occupation, residence and work location, as used in many planning studies. Information about the appreciation of the product, i.e. the shops, the shopping centre and the city in general, is also very important. There may also be some people who live in the city, but shop elsewhere, e.g. commuters who work outside the city (category II). There will probably also be many households living in the surrounding villages and towns, who do not buy their goods in the city but instead in competing shopping centres elsewhere (category IV). It will be interesting to investigate their characteristics and their reasons for not using the city's shopping facilities.

When used in combination with characteristics of usage, demographic and socio-economic variables are important in determining user profiles. These variables have the advantage of being relatively easy to recognise and measure, are usually readily and accurately obtainable from surveys and are also included in many census statistics. In addition they are generally relatively easy to incorporate into geographical patterns and for city marketing the location of the customers is often the single most important usable characteristic in defining target groups. If the customer can satisfy his or her demands at a distance closer to the point of departure, this alternative may often be chosen. For instance, if planners want people living or working in a particular geographical location to use a certain shopping centre, they must be sure there is, among other things, an acceptable access from this centre to both their origin and principal destination locations.

**Understanding the consumer decision process**

It is particularly important for city planners and managers, concerned with encouraging changes in spatial behaviour through city marketing, to understand consumer decision-making. For users of the city, changing shopping, recreation or transport behaviour may require changes in established behaviour patterns, attitudes, and even in life-styles. For non-users of the city, for instance new firms or investors, a new location may involve a great deal of uncertainty, which may only be acceptable if the advantages are clearly seen to outweigh the assumed disadvantages.

There is a vast amount of literature on individual decision-making, much of which is directly relevant to various chapters of this book. In the context of this chapter an important, if obvious, point is that consumers make choices based on their own *perceptions* of reality rather than on reality as defined by city managers. To effect the desired behavioural changes, those engaged in city marketing need to know about the circumstances and criteria that people employ in making decisions relating to their spatial behaviour, as well as the relative importance of these criteria. It is also necessary to know how consumers evaluate information in making these decisions. Evidently, many consumers do not successfully obtain relevant information. Therefore, selecting the most effective means of communication with various market segments is an important task in city marketing and is discussed in length in Chapter 7 in relation to images.

Decision criteria that will affect a consumer's choice, usually fall into five categories:

1.  monetary benefits and costs: for instance, available investment premiums and tax reductions, living costs, discounts, etc.
2.  time benefits and costs: for instance, travel time, waiting time (for getting information, admission, permits, access to public transport/highways), etc.
3.  place benefits and costs: for instance, scenic routes, varied neighbourhoods, convenient signs and street layout, accessible locations, etc.
4.  sensory benefits and costs: for instance, noise nuisance, smell nuisance, overcrowded and dirty streets/public transport, etc.
5.  psychic benefits and costs: for instance, feeling of personal safety, fear of crime, offensive graffiti, approval of colleagues/friends/family, helpful people/officials/shop-keepers, status acquisition or loss, etc.

These criteria can be elaborated in various ways and it is evident that they must be adapted to the market segment under consideration. However, the various costs and benefits should not be examined simply on an absolute basis, but the criteria should always be studied relative to the characteristics of competing alternatives. The question here is always 'which choices do people have?' and 'how might people with a choice between several competing alternatives trade-off the various criteria against each other?'. A careful city market analysis will reveal that different market segments make different trade-offs. In other words, the priorities of consumers in a housing market may differ considerably from the priorities set by consumers in a recreation market. This alone would demonstrate the importance of performing an accurate and relevant market segmentation as part of the city marketing process.

## Competition and potency analysis

In order to assess the qualities of a city, or district within it, from the perspective of one or more target groups a set of systematic evaluation procedures can be used. If the city's product is compared to that of other cities, then a *competition analysis* is undertaken. If the various neighbour-hoods, or even smaller building blocks within a city, are compared with respect to their potency, or attractiveness for a certain target group, then a *potency analysis* results. In both cases, the analyst has to deal with criteria like the ones discussed above. Consequently, recently developed multi-criteria evaluation techniques (MCE techniques) are more suitable as evaluation aids than the more traditional cost–benefit approaches which limit their attention to monetary consequences and quantitative measure-ments (see Shefer and Voogd, 1990).

MCE techniques are designed to handle a large number of criteria of varying importance, expressed in different units of measurement. Even fully qualitative measures, and trade–off or weighting schemes, can be treated by these techniques. They are very useful in classifying the required information in such a way that the choices to be made become much clearer for the decision-making body.

There are many different MCE techniques, but they almost all take as a starting point a matrix which includes the appraisal scores of various alternatives (e.g. zones, neighbourhoods, towns) with respect to a number of criteria (see for an overview: Voogd, 1983).

*Spatial potency analysis*

Spatial potency analysis is a method which has been devised to handle mixed qualitative and quantitative data. Conventional potency analysis through weighted summation of 'hard' numerical scores, as for instance those discussed by Hopkins (1977) and Chapin and Kaiser (1985), impose severe restrictions on the type and quality of data needed. Besides, it is often very difficult to collect missing quantitative data due to poor databases or a lack of time. For these reasons, a new method has been developed to deal with both quantitative and qualitative information,

**Table 4.1** Structure of score matrix for potency analysis

|  | areas | | | | | |
| --- | --- | --- | --- | --- | --- | --- |
|  | 1 | 2 | 3 | 4 | · | etc. |
| criterion a | ++ | + | +++ | + | · | · |
| criterion b | 125 | 75 | 250 | 50 | · | · |
| criterion c | 12 | 8 | 9 | 14 | · | · |
| criterion d | + | ++ | + | +++ | · | · |
| · | · | · | · | · | · | · |
| etc. | · | · | · | · | · | · |

hence enabling potency analysis to be adapted to 'data poor' conditions (cf. Voogd, 1987b).

The point of departure is the definition of the areas (e.g. neighbourhoods or towns) for which a potency analysis should be performed. The characteristics of these areas can be described by means of a given number of criteria. The resulting 'hard' and 'soft' information can be collected in a so-called score matrix, with the following structure given in Table 4.1. Note that these scores can be both quantitative (i.e. numerical values on a so-called ratio measurement scale) and qualitative indications (i.e. expressions on an ordinal or ranking scale). In other words, all areas obtain as many appraisal scores as there are criteria specified.

Developing a set of criteria with which to characterise the areas is always a source of uncertainty in a potency analysis. This uncertainty, though difficult to control, may be minimised by paying attention to the following questions: 'Is the set of criteria chosen complete, that is, fully representative of the concerns of the target groups involved?', 'Do the criteria fully represent and describe the aspect for which they are intended as a measure?', and 'Are the criteria evenly distributed over the various relevant aspects?'. Such questions must, of course, always be open to debate.

The purpose of a potency analysis is to aggregate the various appraisal scores in order to arrive at one general potency score for each area. Obviously, this general potency score depends on the weights related to the various criteria, which again of course depend on the target groups for which the potencies of the various areas are assessed. Weighting is usually seen as a critical activity in evaluation studies. However, modern MCE techniques free the analyst from using pseudo-precise numerical weights for intrinsically imprecise value-judgements. In practice it appears to be much simpler to make a qualitative distinction between criteria: for instance, 'elderly households (a possible target group) prefer a short walking distance from their home to a facility centre (criterion a) above an improvement in the accessibility of the industrial park (criterion b)'. This is a qualitative statement, because it does not say 'how much' the short walking distance is

**Table 4.2**   Structure of output of potency analysis

|               | areas |     |     |     |      |
|               | 1   | 2   | 3   | 4   | etc. |
|---------------|-----|-----|-----|-----|------|
| target group I   | ++  | +   | 0   | ++  | ·    |
| target group II  | 0   | +   | ++  | 0   | ·    |
| target group IV  | +   | ++  | +   | +   | ·    |
| ·                | ·   | ·   | ·   | ·   | ·    |
| etc.             |     | ·   | ·   | ·   | ·    |

preferred above the park's accessibility. Nevertheless, this qualitative statement enables the analyst to rank both criteria; or, in other words, to express a qualitative weighting scheme for the possible target group of 'elderly households'. According to this principle, it is usually quite possible to link one or more qualitative weight sets of the criteria to particular target groups.

Given the qualitative weight sets, reflecting the priorities of target groups, and the factual data included in the score matrix of Table 4.1, a systematic technique should be applied to link both sets of information in order to arrive at the matrix in Table 4.2. (The details of such a technique and the POTENT computer program (Voogd, 1987b) are given in the appendix.) Two different kinds of analysis are distinguished: a relative potency analysis, which only compares between 'real' areas, and an absolute potency analysis, which compares all 'real' areas with an artificial 'ideal' area. Clearly, the results of the absolute analysis are independent of the alternative areas under consideration, whereas the result of a relative analysis always depends on the selection of areas made.

*Competition analysis*

A potency analysis is able to classify areas, such as building blocks, neighbourhoods and cities, according to their potency or attractiveness for certain target groups. This information can be extremely helpful in developing new market–oriented spatial policies. It may also form the basis for a competition analysis of a city. This implies that the competitive situation of a city as viewed from one or more target groups is compared with the actual situation existing in the town. A potency analysis may be very helpful but not strictly necessary. This approach can be illustrated by means of an empirical example (adapted from Bouwers and Pellenbarg, 1989).

It concerns a competition analysis of seven towns in the north-eastern part of the Netherlands, thus all approximately situated in the same region and therefore acting as rivals in attracting new economic activities (see

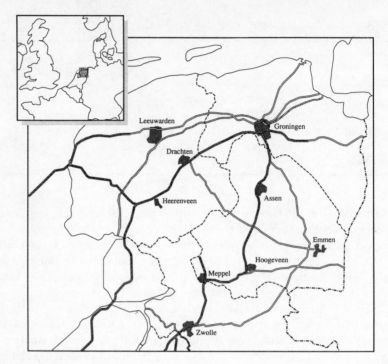

**Figure 4.4** *Competing towns in the North-East Netherlands*

Figure 4.4). The target group is simply defined as 'economic enterprises'. The towns are assessed on the following eight facets or criteria:

A = Qualities of site          E = Attitude of authority
B = Transport infrastructure   F = Commercial contacts
C = Land cost                  G = Residential amenity
D = Possibilities of subsidies H = Labour market

This resulted in the following qualitative score matrix (see Table 4.3). Note that the numbers in Table 4.3 are rankings in which 'higher' is 'better'. It is assumed that the following qualitative weight set appropriately reflects the importance of the various criteria for 'economic enterprises': the most important is criterion A, second criterion B, then equally criteria C, D, E and F, and finally criteria G and H. Performing an absolute potency analysis on this problem defined purely in qualitative terms, results in potency scores in the left hand row of Table 4.5.

These *potency scores* aim at providing a normative description of the factual situation. The other side of the coin, however, are the opinions of the regional 'captains of industry' about the facets/criteria and towns mentioned above. This has been investigated by interviewing a large

**Table 4.3** Score matrix for potency analysis of Dutch towns (adapted from Bouwers and Pellenbarg, 1989)

|  | Towns | | | | | | |
|  | Zw | Ho | He | Dr | As | Em | Me |
|---|---|---|---|---|---|---|---|
| Quality site | 5 | 3 | 3 | 2 | 1 | 1 | 4 |
| Transp. Infra. | 3 | 3 | 2 | 3 | 3 | 2 | 1 |
| Land Cost | 1 | 4 | 3 | 3 | 3 | 2 | 1 |
| Subsidies | 1 | 2 | 3 | 3 | 2 | 3 | 1 |
| Attitude auth. | 1 | 3 | 2 | 2 | 4 | 2 | 1 |
| Comm. contacts | 4 | 2 | 1 | 2 | 2 | 3 | 1 |
| Resid. amenity | 2 | 3 | 2 | 2 | 3 | 2 | 1 |
| Labour market | 3 | 2 | 1 | 2 | 2 | 2 | 1 |

number of entrepreneurs in the region roughly outlined in Figure 4.4. The quantitative results are given in Table 4.4. The scale of the figures in Table 4.4 ranges from –3 (very bad) to +3 (very good). Obviously, the score 0.0 means that the entrepreneurs' judgement was on average 'neutral'. Note that Table 4.4 has a similar structure to Table 4.3, which implies that we can apply the same potency method to this new dataset with a similar qualitative weight set. We will now call the resulting scores *image scores*, because they do not reflect the actual situation, but the situation as perceived by the entrepreneurs. These image scores are included in the right hand row in Table 4.5 (see Chapter 6 for a fuller discussion on images).

Because both the potency scores and the image scores are being standardised to the same measurement unit, we are able to picture the towns in a diagram. The horizontal axis represents the potency scores, whereas the vertical axis denotes the image scores (Figure 4.5). The towns

**Table 4.4** Average opinion scores of entrepreneurs of Dutch towns (adapted from Bouwers and Pellenbarg, 1989)

|  | Towns | | | | | | |
|  | Zw | Ho | He | Dr | As | Em | Me |
|---|---|---|---|---|---|---|---|
| Quality site | 0.5 | 0.0 | −0.4 | 0.4 | −0.1 | −0.7 | 0.1 |
| Transp. Infra. | 1.4 | 0.9 | 0.5 | 0.5 | 0.8 | 0.3 | 0.8 |
| Land Cost | 0.3 | 0.7 | 0.7 | 0.8 | 0.5 | 0.7 | 0.6 |
| Subsidies | 0.3 | 0.6 | 0.5 | 0.6 | 0.8 | 0.8 | 0.3 |
| Attitude auth. | 0.7 | 0.9 | 0.8 | 0.9 | 0.8 | 0.9 | 0.6 |
| Comm. contacts | 1.1 | 0.7 | 0.4 | 0.5 | 0.7 | 0.5 | 0.6 |
| Resid. amenity | 1.2 | 1.2 | 1.1 | 1.2 | 1.3 | 1.4 | 1.1 |
| Labour market | 0.8 | 0.8 | 0.7 | 0.8 | 0.7 | 0.8 | 0.7 |

**Table 4.5**   Absolute potency scores and attitude scores

| Town | potency score | image score |
|---|---|---|
| Zwolle | 0.398 | 0.441 |
| Hoogeveen | 0.463 | 0.439 |
| Heerenveen | 0.206 | 0.000 |
| Drachten | 0.307 | 0.423 |
| Assen | 0.274 | 0.239 |
| Emmen | 0.114 | 0.136 |
| Meppel | 0.000 | 0.159 |

can be represented as points in this two-dimensional space. The dotted line divides the space into two sections: the lower part includes the towns which have a greater potential for economic activities than their image represents (in this example: Hoogeveen, Heerenveen, Assen), whereas the upper part includes the towns with a better image than might be expected on the basis of the potency analysis (Zwolle, Drachten, Emmen, Meppel). In addition, the distance of the points to the origin 0 of the diagram provides some information on the absolute quality of the town in this respect: the larger is this distance, the more 'enterprise quality' the town has. In this illustration, the most attractive towns appear to be Hoogeveen and Zwolle, but note that both towns are still far removed from the highest possible scores of 1.

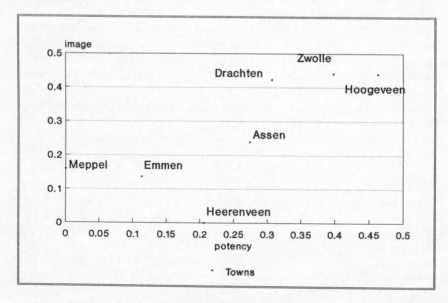

**Figure 4.5**   *Image versus potency of Dutch towns*

**Table 4.6** Example of strength-weakness analysis (adapted from Brouwer and Pellenbarg, 1989)

| | Facets of the town | | | | | | | |
|---|---|---|---|---|---|---|---|---|
| | A | B | C | D | E | F | G | H |
| Potency | +/− | + | ++ | − | + | − | + | +/− |
| Image | +/− | − | + | + | + | + | − | + |
| Therefore: | | | | | | | | |
| Promotion | | * | * | | | | * | |
| Product devel. | | | | * | | * | | * |
| Inaction | *? | | | | * | | | |

A = Qualities of site  
B = Transport infrastructure  
C = Land cost  
D = Possibilities of subsidies  

E = Attitude of authority  
F = Commercial contacts  
G = Residential amenity  
H = Labour market  

*Weakness-strength analysis*

Competition analysis can also be focused on a single town. For example, by comparing the various scores for Hoogeveen, marketing suggestions can be made about the facets under consideration. This is illustrated in Table 4.6, where the first row represents a qualitative interpretation of the potency of Hoogeveen, while the second row represents the image of the town with respect to the facets distinguished. The comparison reveals the necessity for three types of local authority policy response in particular highlighted areas. Where enough facilities or attributes (i.e. potency) exist but are not appreciated or are undervalued by enterprises (i.e. image), then promotion is called for; conversely in the reverse situation a policy for the creation or improvement of facilities is needed: only when the appreciation of attributes and their existence are both positive then inaction may be an appropriate policy response.

*Market-oriented urban models*

The above approaches are particularly helpful in assisting the formulation of short– and medium–term policy. However, policy-making should also take into consideration the strategic, long-term implications of market developments. This may be accomplished through modelling and simulating the behaviour of actors pursuing private ends, but can be constrained by a framework of regulations and physical restrictions because of policy decisions from the past.

There is a vast amount of literature on urban modelling, whether 'urban development models', 'activity-location models' or 'land use models', of relevance to market approaches. Good general introductions and overviews can be found in, *inter alia*, Batty (1976), Chapin and Kaiser (1985), Steiss (1974) and Wilson (1974). It is remarkable that the majority of publications in the field of urban models originate from the 1960s and early 1970s. Due to several reasons (including cumbersome data collection, weak theoretical bases, and inadequate relation with planning practice) the interest in modelling, especially integral urban modelling, flagged since the publication of Douglas Lee's 'Requiem for large-scale models' in 1973. However, there are reasons to believe that interest in market-oriented urban models will increase in coming years, not only because our technical capacity has improved enormously over the last 25 years, but also because theoretical understanding about the functioning of urban systems, the treatment of uncertainties, and the management of data has increased considerably (e.g. see Bahrenberg *et al.*, 1984; Nijkamp *et al.*, 1985; Wyatt, 1989).

Mathematical market-oriented urban models can be very helpful in tracing and simulating market-related urban activity processes. The modelling of urban market processes provides not only a means of testing the practicability of urban land–use alternatives and effectiveness of policy action plans, but it also suggests new avenues for future policy-making in which key market-related considerations are taken into account (see Chapin and Kaiser, 1985).

## Appendix: the program POTENT

### Structure of the input

The computer program POTENT (cf. Voogd, 1987b) performs a spatial potency analysis of a given set of areas or spatial zones i (i=1,2,...,I) whose characteristics have been determined by means of a given number of criteria j (j=1,2,...,J). This information is collected in a so-called score matrix S (of order J × I) with the following structure:

$$(1) \qquad S = \begin{bmatrix} S_{11} & \cdots & S_{1I} \\ \cdot & & \cdot \\ \cdot & & \cdot \\ \cdot & & \cdot \\ S_{J1} & \cdots & S_{JI} \end{bmatrix}$$

where $s_{ji}$ is the appraisal score attached to area i with respect to criterion j. The appraisal scores can be both 'hard' numbers (i.e. numerical values on a ratio measurement scale) and 'soft' indications, for instance in terms of 'moderate', 'bad' or 'good'. For all scores 'higher' means 'better'.

The aggregation of the various scores $s_{ji}$ to a general potency score per area depends on the weights related to the various criteria. These weights, of course, depend on the target group under consideration, and are denoted by the subscript t (t=1,2,...,T). The *weights or priorities* can be denoted formally as a vector $w_t$:

(2) $\qquad w_t' = [\, w_{1t}, w_{2t}, \ldots, w_{Jt} \,]$

The weights can be represented as 'hard' numbers (e.g. on a scale from 0 to 10) or as a 'soft' ranking. For our convenience, we will assume for this moment that the weights are 'hard' numbers, for which condition (3) holds:

(3) $\qquad \sum_j w_{jt} = 1 \quad$ (for all t).

The last section of this appendix shows how qualitative weights can be used.

The purpose of POTENT is to arrive at an aggregate judgement of the potency of the various areas i (i=1,2,...,I) from the perspective of target group t (t=1,2,...,T).

*Methodological structure*

A distinction is made between a *relative* and an *absolute* potency analysis. The approach for a relative analysis will be considered first. A relative potency analysis aims to provide a relative appraisal of the various areas, i.e. the resulting potency score does not provide information about the absolute quality of a particular area: it only reflects the discrepancy with the other areas under consideration.

The criteria j (j=1,2,...,J) are first classified into two sets: a set H containing all 'hard' criteria and a set Z containing all 'soft' criteria. In addition, all areas are pairwise analysed, i.e. for each pair of areas (i,i') two *dominance scores* are calculated, namely a quantitative dominance score o based on the 'hard' criteria:

(4) $\qquad o_{ii't} = \sum_{j \in H} w_{jt} \, (s_{ji} - s_{ji'}) \, (s_{jmax} - s_{jmin})^{-1}$

where:

$$s_{jmax} = \max_i s_{ji}$$

$$s_{jmin} = \min_i s_{ji}$$

and a quantitative dominance score e where is based on the 'soft' criteria:

$$(5) \qquad e_{ii't} = \sum_{j \in Z} w_j t \; (sgn \; [s_{ji} - s_{ji'}] \;)$$

where:

$$sgn \; [s_{ji} - s_{ji'}] \begin{cases} = +1 & \text{if } s_{ji} > s_{ji'} \\ = 0 & \text{if } s_{ji} = s_{ji'} \\ = -1 & \text{if } s_{ji} < s_{ji'} \end{cases}$$

Both dominance scores o and e represent a measure of how much area i has more potency than area i' for the target group t under consideration. However, these scores cannot be compared directly because the measurement units differ. Consequently, a standardisation of both dominance scores is necessary. This results in standardised dominance scores, to be denoted as ô and ê, where:

$$(6) \qquad \hat{o}_{ii't} = (o_{ii't} - o_{tmin}) / (o_{tmax} - o_{tmin})$$

and

$$(7) \qquad \hat{e}_{ii't} = (e_{ii't} - e_{tmin}) / (e_{tmax} - e_{tmin})$$

where tmax and tmin denote the highest and the lowest dominance score respectively for the particular target group t.

By weighting the scores of (6) with the added weights of the criteria of set H and the scores of (7) with the added weights of set Z, and aggregated dominance score $d_{ii't}$ can be calculated:

$$(8) \qquad d_{ii't} = \sum_{j \in H} w_{ji} \, \hat{o}_{ii't} + \sum_{j \in Z} w_{jt} \, \hat{e}_{ii't}$$

In addition, by using (8) a *relative potency score* $p_{it}$ for area i can be determined:

$$(9) \qquad p_{it} = (y_{it} - y_{tmin}) / (y_{tmax} - y_{tmin})$$

where:

$$y_{it} = \sum_{i'} d_{ii't}$$

$$y_{tmin} = \min_{i} y_{it}$$

$$y_{tmax} = \max_{i} y_{it}$$

Obviously, the higher score $p_{it}$ is, the higher potency area i has for target group t.

In an *absolute potency analysis* the area scores are compared to the (theoretically) best possible scores. This implies that, in addition to the pairwise comparison of the 'real' areas discussed before, each area is also compared to a hypothetical 'ideal zone', which is denoted by the index v $(i,i'=1,2,...,I,v)$. Formula (4) changes now into:

$$(10) \qquad o_{ii't} = \sum_{j\in H} w_{jt} (u_{ji} - u_{ji'})$$

where:

$$u_{ji} = \begin{cases} s_{ji}/s_{jv} & \text{if } s_{ji} < s_{jv} \\ 2 - s_{ji}/s_{jv} & \text{if } s_{ji} > s_{jv} \text{ and } s_{ji} < 2s_{jv} \\ 0 & \text{in all other cases} \end{cases}$$

Formula (5) remains unchanged in an absolute potency analysis. It is obvious that per definition $e_{vit}$ equals $_{j\in z}\sum w_{jt}$ under all circumstances. Also the other formulae are used. However, the interpretation of (9) is now slightly different: in case of a relative potency analysis the final potency score will be delimited as in (11), while condition (12) holds for an absolute potency analysis:

$$(11) \qquad 1 \leqslant p_{it} \leqslant 0 \qquad (i=1,...,I)$$

$$(12) \qquad 1 < p_{it} \leqslant 0 \qquad (i=1,...,I)$$

Evidently, in an absolute potency analysis the maximum score of 1 will always be reserved for the hypothetical ideal area v. The further a potency score is removed from 1, the worse the potency of that particular area is.

### The treatment of 'soft' qualitative weights

There are several ways to treat qualitative weights (see also Voogd, 1983). A very straightforward method is to transform a 'soft' ranking of criteria, representing a target group's view, through a so-called expected value method, into the most probable cardinal weight set $E(\mathbf{w})$ (for convenience the index t has been omitted). The following transformation formula can now be used:

$$E(w_1) = 1/J^2$$
$$E(w_2) = 1/J^2 + 1/J(J-1)$$

(13)

$$E(w_{j-1}) = 1/J^2 + 1/J(J-1) + \ldots + 1/J.2$$
$$E(w_j) = 1/J^2 + 1/J(J-1) + \ldots + 1/J.2 + 1/J.1$$

for which it holds that the criteria are ordered such that $w_1 \geqslant w_2 \geqslant \ldots \geqslant w_J$. More technical details about this expected value method can be found in Rietveld (1984).

# 5 Shaping the product

The second major component of the marketing process described in Chapter 3 is the product. The placing of this chapter after rather than before the preceding chapter on the market makes in itself an important initial statement. Markets ultimately create products rather than the reverse. Nevertheless in city marketing, as will be illustrated in various cases later, the urban product can easily be assumed to be given, and the task of the city marketer is only to seek out and capture a suitable market for a pre-existing product. This chapter casts doubt on this assumption and the strategies based upon it.

First, an attempt must be made to answer the question, 'when selling the city, what is actually being sold?' Answers evoke two further questions namely, 'to what extent can this place-product be treated as any other product?', and conversely, 'to what extent does it possess distinctive attributes that require equally distinctive treatment?' Only when these questions have been answered can we proceed to the practical question of, 'how can an urban product, or more usually products, be deliberately shaped by public authorities, in response to the markets outlined in the preceding chapter?'

## What is the urban product?

In beginning to answer this question, it is in many respects easier to be clear about what is not being sold than what is. The textbook definition of a product is 'what a company has to sell', or more broadly, 'anything having the ability to satisfy human needs or wants capable of being traded for some other commodity – for a price' (Kotler, 1986). However, it is clear that the selling of the city, in the sense of this book, is significantly different from the simple archetypal commercial market transaction where a product or service is exchanged for a price. It does not usually involve either the exchange between seller and buyer of ownership over a physical entity, nor even the purchase or hire of any exclusive rights over urban services. London Bridge may have been sold and re-erected in Arizona and

Venetian palazzi now grace cities in Germany, Australia and the United States, but that is not what is normally meant by selling the city. Many such exchanges may occur as a result of the selling of the city, as tourists buy souvenirs or hire hotel beds, but these are ancillary market exchanges that occur after the city has been sold in our sense of the term. Indeed so non-exclusive are the proprietorial rights being exchanged that the use of the term 'selling' may be misleading if too simple an analogy with most commercial market transactions is maintained, and at the very least a broader definition of terms is required.

However, such a dismissal of over-simplification should not be extended to a denial of the validity of the existence of an urban product; only that it is distinctive, multifaceted and in need of careful delineation. As with the entire process of city marketing, the applicability of marketing procedures in planning depends on a redefinition of the components for these new purposes; such a re-examination is particularly and obviously necessary when considering the nature of the product being offered for sale. Successful marketing is unlikely if those trying to do it are unclear about what exactly they are selling.

Any attempt to define the urban product confronts an immediate problem of double meaning. Quite simply the word city, when used in this way, can have two quite distinct meanings. On the one hand, it can refer to the place as a whole, itself a distinct entity formed from physical structures, functions, activities, atmospheres and even symbolic values that somehow become encapsulated in the name of a particular city. On the other hand, it can refer to quite specific services, facilities or attributes that occur at such a place. A 'new town' may be sold to potential industrial investors as a concept, composed of elements such as modernity, enterprise, and efficiency, but also, and often simultaneously, specific attributes, such as cheap building land, fast transport connections, and a neighbouring golf course will be offered for 'sale'. This dualism is more than a terminological confusion that can be clarified by a relabelling of the two meanings; it is deeply entrenched in popular usage and probably inextricable in most marketing exercises.

Sliepen (1988) tried to separate the urban product into two main parts, namely what he termed the *contributory* elements, i.e. specific services or even a particular isolated characteristic of the city, and the *nuclear product* which is the city as a whole. The best that can be done is to be constantly aware of the parallel existence of both meanings and the practical results that stem from this. For example, one important consequence of this dualism in meaning relates to the idea of 'multi-selling' inherent in place commodification, as discussed in Chapter 2. In so far as the city-product being marketed is an 'element' then exclusive rights of usage are more likely to be sold, but in so far as the 'nuclear product' is offered on the market, then the same sets of physical attributes, or even locations in physical space, are being treated as separate products on separate markets.

There are therefore simultaneously both two different urban products, and one product itself constructed of two components.

Such dualism is not unique to city marketing but is found, to a greater or lesser degree, in many other aspects of urban affairs. The city is intrinsically both an entity and a location, a set of attributes and a site, and these two characteristics, although logically distinct, cannot in practice be treated separately.

## Product and resource

All products are constructed from resources of various sorts. The relationship between urban resources and urban products, in particular, can be examined through the example of the production of a specific sort of product in a single urban case.

An urban resource is any attribute or facility of the town that is, or could be in the future, used in the creation of the urban product. Resources are thus demand defined and cannot exist independently from the use made of them. Therefore the same resource may at different times, or in response to different demands made simultaneously upon it, be valued in different ways and used in the shaping of different products. Similarly, although products are shaped from resources, the terms are not synonyms despite being used as such in many urban and regional plans.

Consider, for example, the shaping of an historic city, defined as a product constructed from a selected set of urban historical resources for sale upon a contemporary market (see Ashworth and de Haan (1986) for a discussion of the definition of these concepts). In this case the resources available are a very wide variety of artefacts and attributes that have physically survived, been accumulated in, or ascribed to, this city over time. Thus they could include relict buildings and morphological patterns of streets and spaces, collections of objects with historical values, and associations with historical personalities, events and ideas that have been or could be ascribed to places within the town or to the entire town. The possibilities are thus extremely broad and can be extended even further when it is accepted that the historic value of the resource is defined by the demand for it, not the intrinsic qualities of the resource itself. Historicity has thus no direct connection with authenticity but can equally be derived from legend, literature or folklore or even deliberately staged. The historic product is thus what the market accepts as such. *Heritage* therefore is, like any other urban product, an assemblage of selected resources which in this case are bound together through *interpretation*, i.e. its presentation to customers through various communications media.

In most cities, especially in Europe, the historical resources accumulated over a thousand years of existence, are likely to be numerous, widely spread and extremely varied. Not only is a rigorous selection process inevitable in the shaping of an historical product, but, more significantly, several quite different products can be developed simultaneously. The characteristics of each product are a result of who has performed such a selection, on what criteria and for consumption by which market. Thus it becomes possible to conceive of a whole range of 'historic cities', which are composed of different selections from the same resource base, which may coexist not only within the same city but may overlap in the same physical space. The conservationist, the planner and the tourism manager may each create different urban historic products on the basis of different criteria, for particular user groups.

The idea can easily be extended to other urban products, underlining the important relationship between product and resource that is central to place marketing but distinctly different from the same relationship in more traditional commercial marketing of goods and services.

## Public goods and private goods

What exactly constitutes a 'good' has been subject to considerable discussion and a number of different types have been identified (see Table 5.1). Of particular importance for our purposes is the distinction that is frequently drawn between those goods and services directly subject to market exchange and those that can be termed 'public goods', or 'merit' goods in some North American literature. Thus a 'private good' is traded, i.e. various exclusive rights to its use are transferred from producer to customer at a price determined by open competition between buyers and sellers, while a 'public good' possesses a set of inherent characteristics that render such a transaction either impossible or undesirable. Such a distinction, it should be stressed, is made on the intrinsic nature of the good itself, rather than on the organisational structure or goals of its production or management. Publicly owned organisations frequently trade in private goods, and private firms may, willingly or not, produce public goods. Both a transaction and a price do certainly exist for such goods, through decisions taken about the levels and distribution of fiscal revenues, but these are necessarily at a significant remove from the individual consumption of the particular public product. It is central to this book that public goods exist within markets, however indirectly, and thus the commonly encountered terms 'market goods' or 'market sector' to refer to private goods are particularly misleading.

An understanding of this basic division of the potential urban product is basic to our purposes and its misunderstanding has been responsible for several difficulties which will be encountered later. City marketing, as defined in the preceding chapters, involves the application of marketing approaches to both public and private goods, sometimes separately but more often in various inextricable combinations within packages. The city

**Table 5.1** Various types of products (loosely after Kotler, 1982)

| Good | Example | Exchanged for |
|------|---------|---------------|
| Public goods | Flood control | Taxation |
| Merit goods | Education, health | Zero price |
| Impalpable goods | Status, love | Cash, time, effort |
| Intellectual goods | Information | Cash, effort |
| Political goods | Ideas, issues | Votes, support |

that is being sold is an aggregate of private goods, such as hotel rooms, building land or artistic performances, together with a broad collection of 'pure' public goods (i.e. goods from which extra users cannot by definition be excluded regardless of whether they have paid a price for their use) such as public order or environmental amenity, and various 'impure' public goods (i.e. those whose benefits are subject to irregular spatial distribution for one reason or another) such as subsidised transport, free access road systems or public parks (Pinch, 1985).

## Some guidelines for shaping the product

*Tangible and core products*

The most obvious principle shaping the nature of the product placed on the market can be labelled in general, 'what business are we in?' Although this would be a familiar question posed regularly in commercial organisations, it is much more rarely heard in public sector management operations, where it is too often assumed to be self-evident. These organisations frequently define their task, and thereby the nature of the product they offer, as the effective management of existing facilities, through the efficient operation of current working practices for vaguely defined objectives, rather than constantly reviewing the services on offer in terms of the extent to which they satisfy actual requirements and expectations of existing or potential customers. The management task needs defining in response to the question, 'what actually are customers purchasing?' For example, a municipal bus undertaking will frequently assume that its product is bus rides, whereas what the customer is actually purchasing is transport in accordance with various needs for accessibility, which may or may not be best provided by the existing vehicle fleets and operating practices (see Lovelock *et al.*, 1987). The incremental nature of the acquisition of responsibilities by many public authorities has encouraged a facility orientation. For example, local authorities in many European countries acquired responsibility for the management of swimming baths, often as a result of public hygiene legislation in the nineteenth century: it has only relatively recently become apparent that the public product on offer was not square metres of swimming water which must be efficiently managed, but the provision of a much wider recreational experience through 'leisure pools' and 'recreation centres'. The product has been redefined, in response to customer-based definitions of it, from the hire of swimming space to a package of water related and bankside services which together comprise a recreational product.

The idea that a particular product can be seen at different levels of abstraction is self-evident to any car salesman who variously sells accessibility, convenience, comfort, status or numerous other attributes rather than steel, glass and rubber. The customer is purchasing the *core product*, i.e. a set of valued attributes, through the acquisition of the *tangible product*, i.e. the actual physical product or particular service. Such a distinction has been applied to the marketing by public agencies of tourism destinations by Goodall (1988). He distinguishes, on the one side, the *tangible* aspects of the holiday place-package and the *enhanced* place-product, i.e. the extra services and conveniences included, such as easy payment terms, guarantees, convenient booking systems and the like, from, on the other, the *core* products, such as pleasure, particular life styles, aspired status and other personal satisfaction, that are offered by package holiday destinations.


*Buyer benefit analysis*

The concept of the core product leads to a further step in the analysis, namely that different customers in fact purchase different attributes of the same product. This was introduced in marketing terminology as *buyer benefit analysis* i.e. the attempt to define the product in terms of the benefits the customer is purchasing. For our purposes this approach immediately presents two obvious difficulties. The first is that different customers are likely to be purchasing different benefits through their use of the same product. On the same municipal bus may be commuters purchasing convenient transport, and recreationists purchasing an enjoyable tour; the same service provides different products to different markets. Similarly the city as a whole may be marketed to tourists as historic, to investors as modern, and to residents as rich in amenities. Such product segmentation clearly arrives at a conjunction with the market segmentation through buyer benefits discussed in the previous chapter.

Secondly, and directly relevant to the problem of delimiting the product, is that the service on offer can be envisaged as a whole range of different products, in this sense, at various levels of abstraction. Housing provided as a municipal service is simultaneously offering a set of physical spaces and facilities, the satisfaction of shelter needs, and potentially a location and environment that comprises a complete life-style, for the inhabitants. There are therefore many products on offer to the same customer through the same service and these may well be valued differently by different consumers.

Awareness of this product differentiation is far easier to achieve than quantifying its results. Use in itself is relatively easy to measure but the intent leading to such patterns of use, and buyer benefit analysis requires an understanding of motive, is technically more complicated to investigate.

*Place-product and spatial scale*

One of the intrinsic qualities of places, as discussed in Chapter 2, is that they exist at particular spatial scales, and that different places may coexist within nesting hierarchies. This is a unique characteristic of place-products and has several implications for product definition. First, there is the relationship between products at different levels of the place hierarchy. The marketing of the urban product interacts with that for the local sub–urban, regional and national products: these may reinforce each other, be largely indifferent or contradict and interfere with each other. Indeed in practice it is not so much a question of selection between these three alternative conditions as a continuous and complex oscillation at various times between them.

Secondly, the spatial scale and delimitation of the product being purchased by the consumer may not correspond to that being marketed by the producer. This may occur through the failure of the producer to define the product in terms of the market, through the simultaneous marketing by one producer of a wide variety of products at different spatial scales, or most usually as a result of jurisdictional partitioning. Thus the public authority engaged in selling the city has jurisdiction over, and is responsible to, a legally delineated place, which is unlikely to correspond to the spatial limits of the place being purchased. The tourist's city may be confined to a small area of the historic core containing most of the city's recognisable symbols and attractions, the resident's city may be a much wider amalgam of residential and service districts, while the shopkeeper's city may encompass settlements of potential customers far beyond the legal boundary. The answer to the question, 'what is the place–product to be marketed?' will be complicated in local representative democracies by the question, 'in whose interest is the product being marketed?', and 'to whom are the public producers of the product responsible?'

Clearly the spatial hierarchy of jurisdictions, which is most usually in public sector marketing the product producer or at least assembler, and the parallel spatial hierarchy of places purchased by customers need reconcili-ation by co-operative marketing at the appropriate scale: that is the scale appropriate to the customer. The organisational consequences of this are pursued in Chapter 8, but the implications for product definition can best be appreciated through a particular example.

*Dimensions of the scale problem*    The importance of the scale problem can be illustrated by the case of the Languedoc coast. The 100km long coastline between the Rhône Delta and the Spanish border in south-west France was the subject of a large-scale, long-term, central government sponsored development programme commencing in 1963 (see *Le mission impossible?*, Racine, 1980). The main economic stimulus to revitalisation was the creation of a major coast-based tourism industry centred upon five clusters of resort towns (for the details of this resort development see Pearce, 1981; Murphy, 1985; Ashworth and de Haan, 1987). Research on the nature of the tourism product being marketed by the regional and local authorities, compared with the product being purchased by tourists on the coast has revealed a number of spatial discrepancies (see Stabler, 1988; de Haan, *et al.*, 1990).

On the supply side two distinct spatial scales were being offered on the market.

1.    The regional scale, i.e. the whole coast marketed by the regional development authority as 'Languedoc-Roussillon' on a national, and to lesser extent international market unfamiliar with the region, as a highly generalised package of sun, sand and water sport.
2.    The local scale, i.e. the individual resort as an independent local government 'commune' or as the coastal part of a larger inland commune usually containing a major city. This local product defined by local agencies was usually highly specific in its definition of attractions and targeted at a specialised long-standing local day recreation and second homes demand.

In itself this scale discrepancy created few problems of conflicting marketing strategies as both the producers and the potential customers were themselves spatially distinct and in practice individual resorts were sharply segregated into two groups depending upon these different product definitions. On the demand side, however, a more complicated pattern emerged, with customers defining the tourism product on a larger number of spatial scales, including:

1.    The continental scale, where customers, especially those from outside France, were viewing the coast as an indistinguishable part of a Mediterranean package with a matching set of climatic expectations that the region has considerable difficulty in meeting.
2.    The regional product marketed by the regional authority bears little relationship to the prevailing actual regional product consumed. The 'Mission' promotes the planners' conception of varied but functionally

interrelated resort clusters (the 'unites') set in rural support zones providing informal folklore and natural environmental attractions. The spatial behaviour patterns of visitors and their perceptions of the region, however, largely ignore these characteristics.

3. The purely local, single resort scale, in which local users perceive the product in very restricted spatial terms, purchasing the recreational possibilities of a particular resort, and neither considering nor using the facilities of other resorts or the rural hinterland.

Such variations among both users and producers in the spatial scale of the product has obvious implications and is in part a result of the jurisdictional scale of the various public authorities involved in creating and promoting this particular product, or in reality a set of quite different products. The pronounced discrepancies between the scale of the product which is sold, as opposed to that which is purchased has equally obvious consequences for the effectiveness of the promotional effort. The relative success of the Languedoc-Roussillon coast in attracting recreationists over the last two decades can be attributed mostly to the overall growth in such demands, especially from within the region itself. This, together with a shortage of similar facilities in Mediterranean France, created basically a 'sellers' market' within which the products as defined by the regional authorities were largely ignored, and quite different spatial products, which were mostly unpromoted by official bodies, have been purchased instead.

## Product development

In traditional marketing science there are various other characteristics of the product which occupy much attention but require less consideration in the context of city marketing, at least compared with the important topic of product definition discussed above.

For example, the marketing of commercial products needs to be concerned with the position of an individual product within a complete product line. In city marketing, when the city as an entity is the product, this idea is generally of less relevance and it is not necessary to relate the price, quality or appeal of one product to other products of the same producer. When the city is viewed as a collection of various activities, however, the concept of the related product line may have some relevance as the marketing of any one activity may have an influence upon others of the same city.

Similarly the concept of the product life-cycle, in which a product is seen dynamically to move through a series of phases from development to obsolescence, is less easily applied in this context where the city is the product. However, Butler (1980) has applied this idea to holiday resort towns and linked it to phases of resort growth, stagnation and decline, and such an approach could be more broadly applicable to a wider variety of towns with a similarly dominating and clearly defined function. The variety of urban functions, and thus potential products on a variety of markets, generally renders this approach of less practical relevance to most cities. It is, however, worth noting that quite different marketing strategies are likely to be relevant at different stages in the place-product life-cycle; thus the sort of promotion appropriate for a relatively unknown city on a new market will obviously be quite different from that appropriate for the maintenance or revival of a long–established urban product, and in that sense notice should be taken of the positioning of particular products on such cycles. In addition the nature of the evolution of the product life-cycle is itself strongly influenced by the concept of the product replacement frequency, a frequently replaced product obviously having a quite different life cycle to one infrequently consumed. Such an idea is relevant to city marketing in so far as the different markets for the city can be distinguished in these terms. The place-product offered to visitors, whatever their motive for the visit, is clearly in the first category while the decision to relocate a commercial or residential establishment is equally clearly in the second. Therefore the frequency rate of place purchase, and thus the life-cycle of the place-product, with all the implications this has for new product development and promotion, will depend yet again upon the market definition of the product itself.

The concepts of the product line and product life-cycle lead to the broad topic of product development. City marketing requires not only the identification and definition of the existing urban products, but the devising of strategies for the introduction of new products in relation to the existing product line. This in turn relates to the strategies adopted for the marketing process as a whole. Policies for existing and new products depend upon whether existing or new markets are being targeted. This results in the matrix in Table 5.2, where four general choices are possible, which can be applied to the case of the historic urban product described earlier. A policy of increased market penetration would result in increasing the amount of the existing product sold to the existing market, through perhaps more or extended visitor attractions viewed as retailing outlets for the existing interpreted heritage product. Market development would endeavour to expand the sale of the existing product by attracting new visitors. Product development policies would launch new products, such as adding new historic periods, characters or episodes, to the existing product line. While finally product diversification policies might involve adding different but harmonious products to the urban product line, for example attracting conference visitors or exploiting a local market for historic and cultural services.

Such considerations link the product to the analysis of the market, and product development policy with broader questions of strategy within

**Table 5.2**  Product-market development strategies applied to an historic city

|  | Present product | New product |
|---|---|---|
| Present market | Market penetration (More heritage outlets) | Product development (New interpretations) |
| New markets | Market development (New heritage visitors) | Diversification (New types of visitors) |

market planning. They therefore proceed inevitably beyond the scope of urban product analysis alone and into the content of later chapters.

## The place-product

The simple but persistent conclusion that emerges from all of the above discussion is that a place-product is significantly different from the goods and services for which marketing science was developed. As in all marketing, the product is ultimately defined by the market, by the consumer, but in public sector place marketing this definition is likely to be more complex, because of the mix of public and private goods involved, the dualism inherent in a place as both object and location and in part just because the wide variety of urban resources available allows an equally broad range of potential products to be developed. This inherent complexity is not an excuse for a vague or cursory attention being paid to this aspect of the marketing process: on the contrary it renders product definition even more important in this context than in commercial marketing where frequently the attributes of the product are either self-evident or can be deduced easily from the product's competitive position in relation to the products of other producers. Neither of these conditions is so clearly evident in city marketing.

There is a commonly heard objection that the demand–oriented approach suggested here, however theoretically desirable, is in practice unrealistic. Cities, it is argued, can only sell what they possess and that this possession is very largely the existing physical, environmental, locational, functional and perceptual attributes, which must be taken as largely immutable. This is to confuse the concept of resource with that of product, a misunderstanding that is frequently built in to the organisational structures adopted for place marketing. Departments or agencies are made responsible for marketing a set of place-products which they do not themselves manage, so they may well be reduced to a concentration on promotion and a neglect of those other aspects of the marketing process which are largely beyond their remit.

To conclude that product definition is both different and intrinsically complex in place marketing, leads to the subsequent conclusion not that it should therefore be largely ignored, but that it requires a significantly different form of management as will be discussed in a later chapter.

# 6 Places and place-images

One conclusion that emerges strongly from the preceding chapters is that the definition of the place-product, whether undertaken by the producer or the customer, is heavily dependent on sets of place-images. The potential seller, or purchaser, of a place to live in, work in, invest in or recreate in, depends upon an appreciation of what is expected from the purchase. The characteristics of the place are used to envisage and predict the nature of the place-product and its future use, or for existing customers a validation of current uses. This will be discussed in more detail in this chapter.

## Places, images and marketing

The intrinsic complexity of places, which are aggregations of many varied features and facilities, makes it impossible for either buyer or seller to be aware of, let alone give active consideration to, all but a fraction of the place attributes and their possible uses. A place can only be commodified therefore by means of a rigorous selection from its many characteristics. The results of this selection is the place-image. It is therefore a truism to state that the core of the whole marketing process is the bringing together of products and customer so that exchange occurs, and that the images of place held by the parties to this exchange will determine if, and on what terms, it occurs. In this respect, 'images are more important than tangible resources' (Hunt, 1975, p.1).

Such a declaration of the importance of the topic commits us to an extended investigation of the role of place–images in place marketing but equally opens up an enormous field of investigation. The way individuals perceive and react to their external environment and the way social behaviour is influenced by, and in turn itself influences, attitudes towards places, are central themes of perceptual and environmental psychology and of behavioural sociology. Our trespass in the extensive literature on these topics can be limited by two restrictions. First, our definition of place is necessarily narrower than that of most behavioural scientists, being in practice a selection of a particular spatial scale for the analysis of the

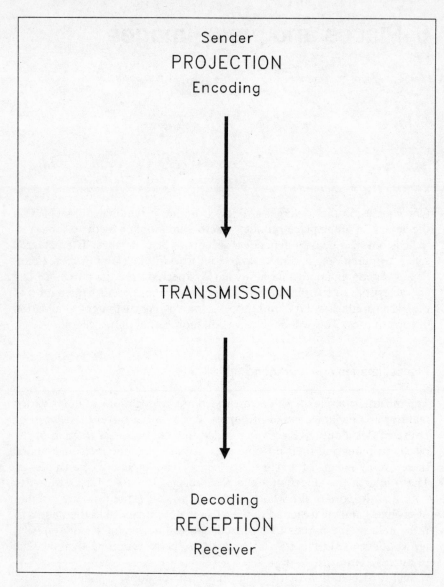

Sender
# PROJECTION
Encoding

# TRANSMISSION

Decoding
# RECEPTION
Receiver

**Figure 6.1**    *A simple model of the stages of image transmission (after Rapoport, 1982)*

environment external to the individual. Secondly, the marketing process is concerned with only one sort of behaviour, namely purchasing behaviour. Although the definition of purchasing was extended in Chapter 2 to include a whole series of actions other than only the direct exchange of products for money, nevertheless our central concern must remain focused upon how the images of places affects the making of deliberate decisions by individuals about their actual use of places.

Even the imposition of such restrictions leaves a wide field of investigation and for our purposes a relatively simple 'radio' analogy (as in Figure 6.1) will be sufficient to help structure this and the following chapter.

It can be envisaged that images about places are *projected*, whether consciously or not, through a set of cultural codes. These are then *transmitted* through a variety of channels, which in itself generally implies some *interference*, distortion or loss of information. Finally individuals are assumed to have *received* messages from external sources, decoded them and used a selection from them in the construction of images.

The coding and decoding stages relate to semiological systems, whereby *'signifier* objects are related to *signified* feelings or states of mind'. Burgess and Wood (1988), for example, have *decoded* place advertising messages about London's Docklands by identifying three sorts of signs contained in advertisements, namely *iconic signs* which represent the referent (such as showing Nelson's Column to indicate London), *indexical signs* which suggest a causal relationship to the receiver (such as traffic sounds which suggest a busy street scene) and *symbolic signs* through which objects can signify by association a wide variety of activities, states of mind or life-styles (such as a brief-case as a symbol of business activity, or a champagne glass for a particular life style). The socio-psychological mechanisms through which this occurs is not our direct concern here (see Uzzell, 1984), but clearly from the point of view of place promotion it is essential that the same semiotic responses are in use by both senders and receivers of messages. Symbolic signs in particular depend for their successful trans-ference on sets of shared cultural values. Place marketing across major cultural differences must be particularly aware of this danger: for example, the promotion of tourism destinations by national agencies on world markets, or the marketing of public services targeted at ethnic minorities in western cities, must clearly use codes appropriate to the culture of the receiver not the producer.

Each of these phases is important to the marketing process and each is considered separately below. However, it needs stressing at the outset that projection, transmission and reception form a logically continuous process and disintegration for purposes of more detailed study creates the very real risk of drawing artificial boundaries through the zones of transition that are precisely the most relevant to our purposes in the entire sequence. Most of the studies described below, however intrinsically interesting, are confined to aspects of either received or projected images and only rarely consider both. Indeed the methods that have been developed for obtaining inform-ation on, and describing the resulting images of, each of the three phases are typically quite different and therefore not comparable, which diminishes their value for the purposes of understanding the specific role of place-images in marketing, and subsequently the effectiveness of deliberate intervention in creating or changing such images.

This chapter will consider the most relevant of the images held by actual or potential users of places. The following chapter will investigate the projection and transmission of place-images, and especially their deliberate projection or image promotion, which is a central instrument of marketing as a goal-directed activity. This is of course to begin at the end rather than the beginning of the process. Although strictly illogical, it can be easily justified for our purposes. Image promotion, in particular in city marketing, is only very rarely the creation of new images in a perceptual vacuum: it is far more usually the accommodating, modifying or exploitation of existing images, derived from a wide variety of sources over which marketing has little or no control (see also Voogd, 1989b). The receiver is not a passive victim of incoming messages which immediately affect existing images and thereby behaviour: effective promotion requires 'active collusion' (Uzzell, 1984), itself a consequence of pre-existing dispositions.

Indeed promotion as a marketing strategy, as is clear in most of the cases discussed in Chapter 8, is most likely to be employed once it has become abundantly clear that the existing place-images are so negative as to hinder the achievement of management objectives. If existing place-images are positive or even barely existent there is in practice little incentive to promote, so that most of the promotion discussed in the following chapter is remedial and corrective. It can be argued in relation to Western cities in particular that a long–standing popular anti-urban bias, whose origins may be traced to nineteenth-century romanticism, has been constantly reinforced by public media reporting of problems in cities, so that all city marketing starts with a promotional handicap. Thus it is essential to begin with an understanding of the place-images that exist together with factors that influence them, and only subsequently to proceed to the means of modifying them.

## The study of environmental images

Despite the central importance of images in the marketing process and a substantial literature on their use, it is nevertheless difficult to define and therefore analyse their characteristics with any precision. However, a number of academic disciplines have been concerned with different aspects of environmental images and have made contributions which can be useful here.

The attention of the environmental psychologists has been principally focused upon the sensory perceptions of the individual of specific environmental situations and the resulting behavioural reactions to these (see Hall, 1969, and Mercer, 1971, for an overview of research into the reaction of people to various spatial situations). The nature of the conclusions have usually been either too generalised in their definitions of environmental characteristics (such as behavioural reactions to overcrowding) or paradoxically too clinically specific to individual psychological disorders, to be

**Table 6.1**  Place images in the decision-making process (modified from Goodall, 1988)

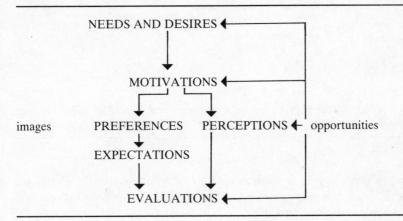

of direct use for our purposes which are distinguishing the image of one particular place from another, and recognising and explaining the differences between images of the same place. The attention of most of the literature in marketing science on the other hand is focused upon measuring the effectiveness of the transmission of particular place-images, but this concentration upon effectiveness, itself determined by monitoring changes in consumer behaviour, understandable given the origins of marketing in the commercial sector, makes the study of the images themselves of secondary importance.

The central role of images within behaviour can be simply summarised by Table 6.1. An individual's existing needs and desires contribute towards the shaping of motivations. Then follows the process of selection from the alternatives existing in the available opportunity set. Information is received upon a portion of these opportunities and an 'evaluative image' formed. This image is then compared with the 'preferential image' derived from the potential consumer's motivations. This comparison forms the basic instrument for selection or rejection of the new information. In practice of course such a linear critical path becomes circular as the experience of the actual consumption leads to measures of satisfaction which in turn influence the perceptions of the opportunity set as well as the preferences and expectations of the consumer.

Such a model demonstrates the importance of information processing in the mind, but contributes nothing towards explaining how this occurs. Cognitive psychologists have suggested the existence of the process shown in Table 6.2, in which there is a triangular relationship between objective reality, in our case places, the individual's explorative behaviour of that reality through perception, what we could term place experience, and the

**Table 6.2**  The perceptual cycle (modified from Neisser, 1976)

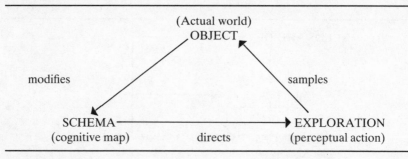

existing 'schema' (see, for instance, Rao and Farley, 1987). These are cognitive structures that prepare the perceiver to accept kinds of information, having therefore an anticipatory as well as a classificatory function. These schemata have a central role within the perceptual cycle as an information accepting system, selecting and processing the stream of perceptions obtained about places and thereby directing exploratory behaviour to sample more information from objective reality. Place-images are schemata in this sense, being both passively modified by information as well as actively controlling the process of its selection.

It might reasonably be expected that the academic discipline with the strongest inherent concern for analysing this aspect of the relationship between people and the environment would be geography, which has long claimed this interface as its subject area and which in addition is inevitably synthetic in the sense of recognising the synthesis of widely diverse features of places as the object of analysis. However, despite these predispositions, it is remarkable that the mental images of places were effectively neglected by geographers until relatively recently in favour of a search for objectively measurable aspects of the reality of places. Although references to the more abstract 'character' or 'atmosphere' of places can be found in much regional geography, sometimes being raised to the level of a semi-mystical ingredient of the character of the French 'pays' or German 'landschaft', it was not delineated but emerged more through intuition than analysis, and both its origins and its effects remained uninvestigated. Although the concept of 'cognitive map' was introduced by Tolman in 1948, writers such as Lowenthal (1961), Lynch (1960) or Tuan (1974; 1975) had to preach with a missionary fervour for the acceptance of the images of places as a valid object of study against a professional mainstream that distrusted the scientific credentials of imagination as an instrument for understanding places. Twenty years' development has resulted in a substantial literature, (summarised in, among others, Gould and White (1974), Downs and Stea (1973), Pocock and Hudson (1978), and Saarinen *et al.*, 1984) which apart from giving credibility to the study of place-images has contributed some methods of description of their attributes, despite the major stumbling block of finding objective techniques suitable for the measurement of subjective reality.

There is no necessity to duplicate much of this previous work here, but it can be drawn upon for the provision of some working definitions and classifications. An image as, 'the sum of direct sensory interaction as interpreted through the observer's value predispositions' (Pocock and Hudson, 1978, p.19) places the stress on interpretation through an individual's values. Others have attempted to broaden perception and to list some of its results. 'An image may be defined as the sum of beliefs, ideas and impressions that a person has' (Crompton, 1979a, p.18), or it is 'an individual's beliefs, impressions, ideas and evaluations' (Burgess, 1982, p.2), or 'the learned and stable mental conceptions that summarise an individual's environmental knowledge, evaluation and preferences' (Walmsley, 1988, p.36). The common ground of almost all this literature is that images are formed from an amalgam of a wide variety of perceptions, in the sense of interactions rather than only visible sensory impulses, of the individual on the world as filtered through the existing personality constructs. Further refinement of the nature of these interactions and constructs is rarely attempted, would lead too far from the central concern here, and is in any event not necessary for our purposes.

However little is known about how exactly they are formed, it is nevertheless possible to recognise different components within images that have practical value for marketing purposes. Images may be, according to Downs and Stea (1973), *denotative* (i.e. denoting something) or *connotative* (i.e. effecting behaviour) or, more usually in marketing contain elements which are *designative, appraisive* and *prescriptive* (Pocock and Hudson, 1978) which are mixed in different proportions in different place-images, which in turn lead respectively to an individual's classifications, valuations and judgements about places. Similarly the relationship between the image and the objective realities of places can be summarised as partial, simplified, idiosyncratic and distorted (Walmesley, 1988). The congruence of the image with reality can range along a spectrum from the over-simplification of *stereotypes*, which can become systematised into *myths* and then become unresponsive to change as *prejudices* (Allport, 1954). Why and how this occurs is of less importance here than describing the nature and extent of this partiality and simplification, generalising about the distribution of this idiosyncracy among identifiable consumer groups, and appreciating and possible ultimately influencing the extent of this distortion.

## Received images of places

From the point of view of marketing the reception of place-images by intended target groups, and consequent changes in customer behaviour, is the final phase in promotion. However, as pointed out earlier, the targeting of specific segments of markets rarely achieves this implied degree of precision and most received images are derived largely from unintended projection. Therefore, promotion has to be aware of, and thus accommodate, the pre-existing images and the existing cognitive structures which prepare the perceiver to accept, reject or modify the messages promoted (Neisser, 1976).

There has been substantial research on the nature and consistency of these images which has generally either tried to relate various image components to a range of demographic, social or spatial characteristics of those holding them, or attempted to analyse the contents of the images held by specific consumer markets. Some of the earliest studies of the mental maps of cities held by individuals concentrated upon differences in the way places were imagined and subsequently expressed through the recognition or reproduction of their spatial characteristics. Commonly researched attributes of the receiver have been age (for example the many studies of the perceptions of distance and direction held by school children (Haddon, 1960; Pocock and Hudson, 1978; Hart, 1984) or students (Saarinen, 1973), and ethnic or cultural characteristics (Lynch, 1960). To these have been added many other variables including gender, levels of educational attainment, accustomed patterns of mobility, and location of place of residence. All have been demonstrated to be important variables in establishing the extent, and the amount and type of detailing of the mental maps held by individuals. Numerous approaches were used of which one of the earliest was cognitive mapping (described at length in various studies in Downs and Stea, 1973) and content analysis of verbal messages through semantic differentials, both of which are essentially descriptive techniques. Others, however, included multivariate and repertory grid techniques which attempted to link the sets of attitudes held by individuals, their 'personal constructs' with their expressed images of the environment (Harrison and Sarre, 1978; Riley and Palmer, 1976).

The accent throughout in such studies was upon intra–urban character-istics, described cartographically or verbally, rather than upon general images of the city as a whole in comparison with other cities. An extension of these attempts at describing the dimensions of the place-image was the description of preferences either between or within cities. A number of national 'opinion geographies' have been constructed on the basis of potential choices of holiday, investment or residential locations. Figure 6.2 (Monheim, 1972) shows a typical example of this method of ascribing preferences to cities for particular purposes in Germany. Similarly qualitative judgements upon attributes of places have also produced a number of local scale 'geographies' of the perceived attributes of places at various spatial scales. Milgram and Jodelet's (1976) account of opinions on the residential desirability of the various arrondissements of Paris, or the detailed mapping of fear in the inner city of Groningen (Figure 6.3] in

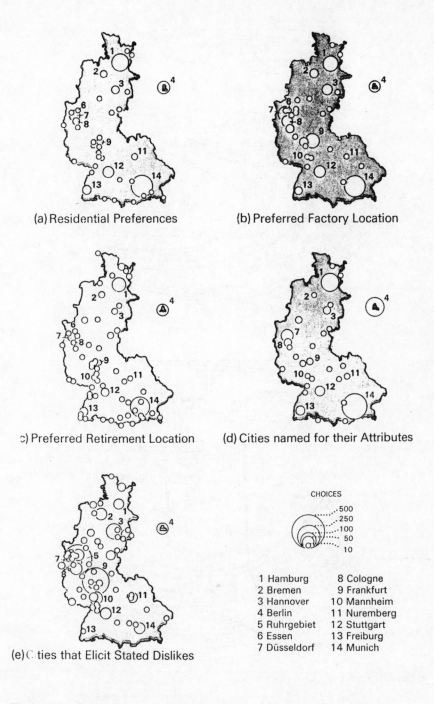

(a) Residential Preferences

(b) Preferred Factory Location

c) Preferred Retirement Location

(d) Cities named for their Attributes

(e) Cities that Elicit Stated Dislikes

CHOICES

500
250
100
50
10

1 Hamburg
2 Bremen
3 Hannover
4 Berlin
5 Ruhrgebiet
6 Essen
7 Düsseldorf
8 Cologne
9 Frankfurt
10 Mannheim
11 Nuremberg
12 Stuttgart
13 Freiburg
14 Munich

**Figure 6.2**  *City preferences in West Germany*

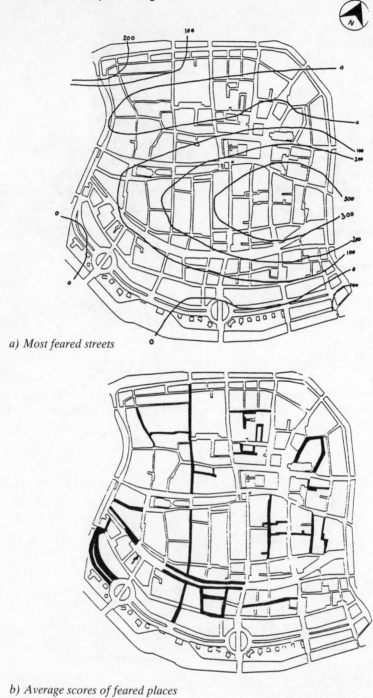

*a) Most feared streets*

*b) Average scores of feared places*

**Figure 6.3**   *Micro geography of fear in Groningen*

relation to various physical and functional features (Alteren, 1989), will serve as examples.

The utility for our purposes of this extremely large, and still rapidly growing body of work is limited partly by the familiar difficulty of an absence of agreed definitions, terminology, methods of data collection and measurement. Even studies of the same image components among populations with similar attributes can rarely be aggregated so that widely applicable generalisations can be drawn. In addition marketing is essentially concerned with changes in attitudes and thus behaviour. Very few of these studies go beyond the description of the images held by particular groups at a chosen moment. How and in what way place-images change, or can be changed, can usually only be incidentally deduced. Particularly instructive therefore are studies such as Pearce (1977; 1981b) on the way travel experience elsewhere left what he termed 'mental souvenirs', which affected the stereotypes held of Australian cities, or more generally estimates of the influence of experience abroad on attitudes to home environments.

The second line of investigation, in contrast to the above, involves the assumption of consistency in the personal characteristics of the receiver but variation in the places being investigated. Different places can then be evaluated against each other in terms of their accepted images for particular purposes rather than against variations in the characteristics of the consumers. These approaches have proved particularly attractive for promotion purposes and a large number of such studies have been produced for different markets, a selection of which will be discussed below.

One of the major problems of most of these studies is the difficulty of obtaining adequate control groups. Research into tourist destinations, for example, generally seeks to describe the images of actual visitors; similarly, studies of residents or investors in particular places can most conveniently question the actual users for these purposes. Those who have chosen not to visit, live, work or invest in a particular place also have images, however, presumably vague or even negative ones, but these prove in practice very difficult to investigate. A notable, albeit small-scale, exception was Dietvorst's (1987) study of some necessarily rather generalised aspects of the images held of the city of Nijmegen in the Netherlands by a randomly selected sample of the national population, regardless of whether respondents had a first-hand experience of the city. Such studies avoid the problem of measuring only the results of success and not those of failure, assuming that actual existing users will have more favourable images than non-users. They provide a useful basis for future promotional exercises by outlining the nature of the image problems to be overcome and the sort of resistance to be encountered among potential targets.

Of the many possible ways of structuring the place–images held by individuals, the most logical for marketing purposes is by the uses to which

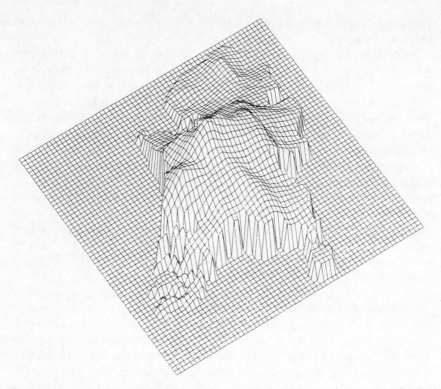

**Figure 6.4**   *Images of entrepreneurs in the Netherlands*

places are put. The most important of these can now be grouped under three general headings: entrepreneurial images, residential images and tourist images.

*Entrepreneurial images*

As much of the earliest conscious effort of public authorities in the field of promotion was directed towards the attraction of exogenous private investment, the image of places held by potential commercial investors has been of obvious importance. One of the few long-term national scale studies is that of Pellenbarg *et al*. (1985) and Meester and Pellenbarg (1986) which concentrates upon the description of the spatial variations in what they term the *enterprise climate* of the Netherlands, itself composed of two elements, the *production environment*, i.e. the totality of circum-stances of a place that are perceived as being important in the production process by entrepreneurs, and the *informational environment*, i.e. the content and nature of actual flows of information about places received by entrepreneurs. This investigation examines the attitudes held by nationally derived samples of commercial entrepreneurs and managers of the various regions of the country as a whole. Its wide scope is intended to allow the creation of national surfaces from the general characteristics which render places attractive for commercial investment in the minds of a restricted but nationally distributed group of decision-makers. The type of results obtained can be seen in Figure 6.4 in which the collective images are scored and plotted as trend surfaces.

These raise, inevitably given the coverage, problems of scale in that many substantial intra-regional variations are averaged away, despite the considerable differences that exist even in a small and socially unified country such as the Netherlands. An illustration of a particularly interesting discrepancy raised earlier was that the regions as perceived did not correspond to the actual existing political and statistical collection regions, and thus to many of the jurisdictional units that are engaged in place-image promotion. Similarly substantial differences in the national map of perceptions were revealed according to the region of origin of the perceiver. Thus the home region of the potential investor was an important variable in shaping the image of the production environment (Figure 6.5), and of particular relevance to regional economic support policies was the considerably less favourable view of the national periphery held by the 'centre', from which most national public and private investment might be expected to originate, than the view from within the peripheral regions themselves (see Voogd, 1989b). These studies bear a clear similarity in technique and national scale with the residential preferences of Gould and White (1974).

The broad scope of this work into investors' images leaves two aspects for further investigation. Given the necessity for a national sample, the place-images themselves can only be described in very generalised terms using such categories as accessibility, local attitudes to work, general environmental amenity, local 'civic cultures' and the like. Secondly, local variations, which in practice include the city scale, tend to be overwhelmed by such broad brush treatment: whole regions of the country are seen by investors from elsewhere in terms that apply only to a small part of it. This can be justified when dealing with exogenous investment where such images are appropriate, but, as has been stressed earlier, intra-regional investment, including the maintenance of existing local investment, depends upon much more detailed local images.

Examples of such local investigations are relatively rare, given the importance of such local financial decision–making (see Lukkes, 1988a). Boogholt and ter Hark (1988) have described in detail the Dutch city of Groningen as perceived by existing and potential entrepreneurs; while in the same region the much smaller town of Hoogeveen was investigated by Pellenbarg *et al*. (1988) and the valuations of the town's effectiveness in the provision of various urban services was measured for a range of different user groups.

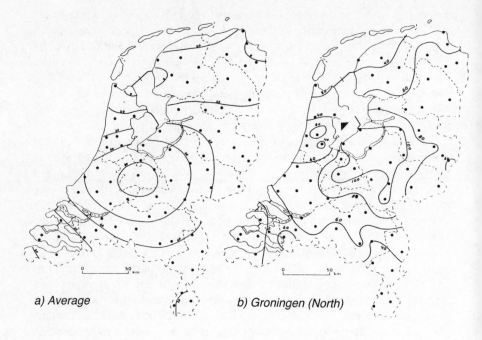

a) Average

b) Groningen (North)

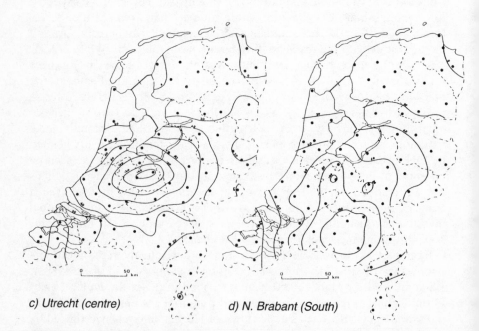

c) Utrecht (centre)

d) N. Brabant (South)

**Figure 6.5** *Variations in the image held by entrepreneurs according to place of residence*

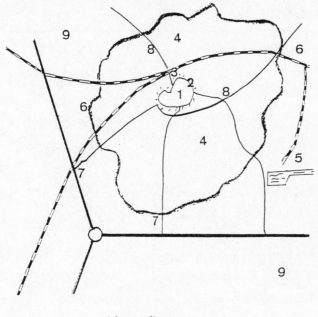

1 Inner city
2 Edge of Inner city
3 Railway Station
4 Residential areas
5 Harbour/Heavy industrial area
6 Light industrial area
7 Office park
8 Approach roads
9 Outer city

**Figure 6.6**   *Locational preferences within cities*

A quite different approach is the descriptive modelling of locational preferences within an idealised city. This has been attempted by Lukkes (1988b) using a national sample. The locational categories shown in Figure 6.6 are used to compare the present and preferred locations of actual commercial firms within specified cities (Table 6.3).

*Residential images*

The values placed upon various qualities of residential environments was investigated for a national sample in the Netherlands by Cramwinckel and

**Table 6.3**  Present and preferred locations of commercial activities in cities
[After Lukkes, 1988]

a)  Present and desired locations

|  |  | Desired Location | | | | | | | | |
|---|---|---|---|---|---|---|---|---|---|---|
|  |  | 1 | 2 | 3 | 4 | 5 | 6 | 7 | 8 | 9 |
|  | 1 | 36 | 10 | 4 | 1 | 0 | 16 | 21 | 14 | 4 |
|  | 2 | 2 | 25 | 9 | 1 | 4 | 7 | 15 | 15 | 3 |
|  | 3 | 1 | 2 | 10 | 0 | 2 | 4 | 8 | 4 | 1 |
| Present | 4 | 2 | 2 | 1 | 9 | 6 | 14 | 15 | 5 | 1 |
| Location | 5 | 1 | 1 | 0 | 0 | 45 | 7 | 7 | 4 | 1 |
|  | 6 | 0 | 5 | 3 | 0 | 19 | 156 | 61 | 21 | 13 |
|  | 7 | 0 | 2 | 4 | 0 | 1 | 6 | 83 | 8 | 0 |
|  | 8 | 2 | 3 | 4 | 1 | 1 | 8 | 33 | 43 | 1 |
|  | 9 | 2 | 0 | 0 | 0 | 5 | 13 | 11 | 4 | 29 |

[Numbers refer to map locations in figure 6.6]

b)  Desired locations as percentage of present locations

|  | Present | Desired | % |
|---|---|---|---|
| Centre | 106 | 46 | 43 |
| Edge of centre | 81 | 50 | 62 |
| Station | 32 | 35 | 109 |
| Residential area | 55 | 12 | 22 |
| Heavy industry area | 66 | 83 | 126 |
| Light industry area | 278 | 231 | 83 |
| Office park Randstad | 104 | 254 | 244 |
| Approach road | 96 | 118 | 123 |
| Outer area | 64 | 53 | 83 |
| Total | 882 | 882 | 100 |

Nelissen (1989) in such a way that the profile obtained of particular towns could be compared with a national average. It is understandable that residents and tourists will tend to hold quite different images of the same places. Residents have different information sources, most especially their own first-hand daily experiences, and have quite different patterns of expectation and use. The nature of some of these differences was examined on a national scale in the Netherlands by Heida and Gordijn (1978). A more detailed city study in Hull (Burgess, 1974) used the simple expedient of asking samples of visitors and residents to typify the town as a whole in terms of sets of adjectives. The results, not unexpectedly, demonstrated that the images of visitors were decidedly more stereotyped, that is they tended to assign Hull to some broadly defined class of city on the basis of a few simple characteristics; in this instance it was frequently seen as a Northern English industrial town, with all the associations this conjured up drawn from sources as wide as the novels of Dickens and television programmes such as Coronation Street. Residents conversely tended to ignore, or take for granted, such general typologies and saw instead the more variegated contrasts between Hull and other towns in the region or with a similar history of economic development. Subtler characteristics were captured in the more finely drawn frame of reference of residents. The second major and related contrast was in the selection of notable attributes. Visitors tended to ignore what they saw as ubiquitous, such as shops, buses or parks in favour of the more distinctive, such as the port. Residents conversely tended to focus on just these ubiquitous characteristics overlooked by visitors and passed judgements on the town according to the perceived quality of such facilities and amenities.

A disadvantage of such studies is that the images of the town held by existing users are likely to be different from non-users, if only because the former have already made a decision and may seek *post hoc* justifications for it. The Hoogeveen study (Pellenbarg *et al.*, 1988), described in Chapter 3 as an example of a market plan, avoided in part this difficulty by investigating the valuations of previous as well as current residents, although the images of future or potential residents was still excluded.


*Tourist images*

The central importance of place-images in the promotion of tourism destinations has already been argued. It must be stressed again here that there are structural characteristics inherent in the nature of visitors as against residents, but also in both tourism as a recreational activity and as a commercial industry that renders visitor destination images critical to the whole marketing process. Schmoll (1977) has listed some of the peculiarities of tourism as a commercial activity including, on the supply side, the diverse nature of the product, the existence of large numbers of small enterprises contributing to the final product, the role of co-ordinating intermediaries in both the private and public sectors, and the perishability and non-storability of the product. On the demand side, can be added the varied and complex motives for travel. Despite many different explanations sought in social psychology (e.g. Dann, 1976, 1978, 1981; Crompton, 1979a; Pearce, 1981a; Uzzell, 1984), there is an underlying agreement that tourism is 'society's' institutionalised means of enabling fantasy and reality to be imperceptibly mixed' (Uzzell, 1984, p.85). In pursuit of such personal satisfaction the customer is compelled to choose between a wide range of alternative destinations on the basis of extremely limited information, and an infrequency of purchase which limits the acquiring of such information through first-hand experience. Thus a market is created which is typified by a fashion-conscious volatility being prone to rapid and dramatic shifts in response to changes in information. The producer of the tourism destination product is thus not only especially vulnerable to changes in the image held of the reality of the destination, but also presented with a particular opportunity to manipulate this relationship of reality and fantasy that is so central to the tourism experience.

The modelling of the decision-making process through the cone of narrowing choices shown in Kent's (1990) tourism consumer model (Figure 6.7) conceives of sets of holiday opportunities being constructed from the total of all possible holidays according to two dimensions, namely what is known to the potential consumer *(perceived set)* and what is seen as realisable (*attainable set*) within such constraints as cost, time or distance. A chain of selections then occurs until a final single choice emerges. The perceptions held of the destinations are of crucial importance in two ways. First, they determine the delimitation of both the perceived and attainable sets; the former by definition is composed of what is known but also the latter is very largely delimited by what is perceived as being attainable. Secondly, each of the decision-making processes makes use of images of the destination although in different ways, a point of obvious importance to those attempting to influence such decisions through promotion.

It is not surprising, therefore, that the images held of places as potential tourist destinations should have received a disproportionate amount of attention in the academic literature. These studies generally fall into two broad categories: they are either a description of the views of one national customer sample on a variety of destinations or a comparison of the images of various international customers of a single potential holiday destination.

Dilley's (1986) investigation of the way Canadians viewed various potential overseas holiday destination countries is an example of the first. Such studies usually concentrate on the explanation of variations in terms of the characteristics of the respondents, especially holiday motivation and previous experience. A more detailed comparative study of competing national destinations in a particular market, in this case the Dutch package tour market, is van Dijk's (1990) descriptions of images of various Eastern Mediterranean countries as holiday destinations. Discrepancies emerged between the images of those dependent completely on second-hand information and those with direct experience of the destinations concerned and, even more dramatically, between those held by potential customers and those projected by the destinations themselves.

The second approach is the study of the way customers from different national markets view a single destination. In practice it is these images that have the most direct relevance to national tourism agencies, who use them as a basis for the devising of promotional strategies. An example is the Dutch National Tourist Office (NBT, 1986) analysis of the way the

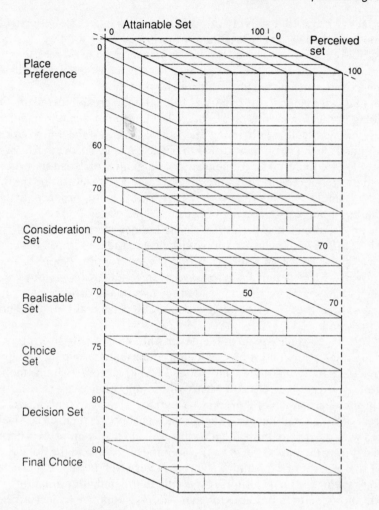

**Figure 6.7** *Selection sets of holiday destinations* (Kent, 1990)

main existing national groups of visitors had distinct expectations of the Netherlands as a holiday destination and translated these into equally distinctive patterns of behaviour. The size of the respondent sample needed in such investigations tends to result in such highly generalised terms as 'historic', 'beach oriented' or 'beautiful landscapes' used to describe whole national tourism products. Crompton (1979a) has attempted to examine in more detail the effects of the two variables of distance and time upon a single national holiday destination, namely Mexico, for its largest single foreign market, which is the United States. The result was a convincing demonstration of the distance-decay effect, in that the longer the destination-market distance the less detailed and more generalised the image. He also traced a stability of national images over time, effectively regardless of changes in the destination, although such stability was not necessarily reflected in tourism behaviour as the customers' reactions to such images remained volatile. However, it does emphasise the difficulty of altering existing entrenched images through promotion.

The study of regions and localities can attempt greater detail in the describing of the dimensions of the image but encounter a major sampling problem. The difficulty of obtaining the control sample of the non-visitor is compounded when attention is turned to particular specific locations. Most such studies are undertaken for convenience among actual visitors, whose first-hand experience will contribute towards a detailed view of the destination. A sample of non-visitors however is likely to produce highly generalised or non-existent images of such specific places.

An early national comparison of local holiday destinations was the English Tourist Board's classification of English seaside resorts on the basis of their popular image on a spectrum that ranged from the 'sophisticated' to the 'lively'. More detailed studies have been conducted at various times over the last 20 years by particular tourist towns among existing visitors in a number of countries as more or less routine and generally unpublished market research.

The role of the spatial scale in the destination images held by visitors is especially interesting, and is especially important in determining the most affective scale for promotion. The Goodall (1988) customer choice model (Figure 6.8) suggests a series of scales whose importance alters with the stage in the decision-making process. A national destination is chosen on the basis of a national image, a region and locality are then successively selected with the help of more detailed images, and finally more local detail is added during the period between the booking decision and the holiday as part of the process of expectation. This may very well be the sequence of decision-making for many visitors, especially to unfamiliar destinations, or indeed, and equally important, for many non-visitors who reject further investigation of national opportunities at the first stage because of an unattractive national image. To repeat Goodall's example a potential tourist whose national image of Ireland is dominated by fears of uncertain personal security will not be receptive to information on particular regions or resorts.

However, the holiday images at different spatial scales may not always contribute to such a straightforward decision 'tree'. The case of the series of seaside resorts along the coast of Languedoc-Roussillon in Southern France was described in Chapter 5 as an illustration of the way quite different products were defined at different spatial scales. It is also notable here that the images of each scale held by holiday makers differed not only in content but in amount of detail (Ashworth and de Haan, 1987). Visitors had a clear and strongly held preference for particular resorts which they saw as distinctive places offering a distinctive holiday experience, and it

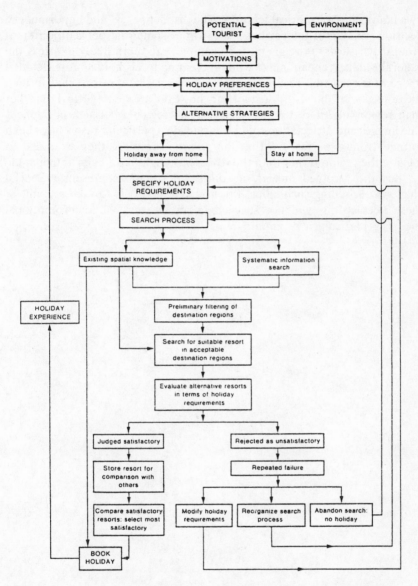

**Figure 6.8**　*Consumer choice model of holiday destinations* (Goodall, 1988)

was this local scale that was the most important in influencing the location of the holiday and the activities undertaken. The region as a whole on the other hand was seen in very general terms which could relate to the Mediterranean coast as a whole. What was even more surprising is that the resort-region was seen as largely an extension and reflection of the resort itself, being endowed with the characteristics of the resort rather than its own landscape or historical features. The distinctiveness and importance in decision–making of the various scales varies somewhat between different groups of visitors. Foreigners, for example, are more likely to stress the general Mediterranean image while recreating locals hold a more detailed image of a particular resort, or even a beach within a resort, that formed the objective of the visit. Most visitors however are resort-attracted rather than region-attracted, perhaps because the regional decision is implicit. The images and expectations of places outside a particular resort have been formed from experience within the resort. These are then extended to include the region rather than the reverse as might have been anticipated.

Thus the received images of tourism destinations present a special challenge in selling such cities. Promotion which fails to take account of these peculiarities will not succeed in an industry where promotional success is particularly essential.

# 7 Image building and the promotion of places

Places can be marketed through their generalised images even though the goods and services being sold are difficult to specify. Image building is therefore an important and widely used means of intervening in markets. However, the shaping and projection of suitable urban images can seldom be limited to producing four-colour brochures and catchy slogans. As will be discussed in this chapter at length, the transmission of images is a complex and difficult process that needs a sound prior understanding of the urban product, the target groups under consideration and the means of communication between them.

## The nature of place promotion

The obvious central role of promotion in the whole marketing procedure, in relating the product to the market, has led to it being, on occasion, equated with marketing itself rather than being viewed as just one part of a wider process. Such a statement as, 'the promotion is the product, the brochure is the package' (Jefferson and Lickorish, 1988), although a distortion of marketing as presented earlier, is an accurate description of practice, in this case in the package tourism industry. Such an understandable exaggeration is particularly evident in the marketing of places where, as a result of the peculiarities of product and market discussed in previous chapters, marketing can too easily be reduced to little more than disembodied promotional exercises. Promotion can be defined simply enough as comprising, 'all communication measures designed to create awareness of, interest in, and a favourable image for, existing or new facilities or services with the aim of attracting customers to them' (Schmoll, 1977, p. 8). Few would dispute such a general definition but each of its constituent elements needs closer examination, especially when applied to places.

It should be stressed at the outset that, although promotion is a communication activity, not all communication is necessarily promotion, only that which is undertaken with the clear objective of influencing the behaviour of those at which it is targeted. Much, probably most, of the information being promoted about places, in the general sense of the definition above, either has no such purpose in mind or is motivated by such vaguely defined purposes, as hardly to qualify as an activity designed to influence behaviour in a predetermined way. Almost all users of places have an enormous existing store of information, feelings and expectations about places, acquired and structured as described in the preceding chapter, which is being continually supplemented by a myriad of information sources, very few of which are intended to influence specific consumer behaviour in a predetermined purposeful way.

Promotion, in the specific goal-directed sense used here, makes only a small contribution to this store of information, which also emanates from first-hand experience, face–to–face verbal communications of friends and acquaintances, and the news and entertainment media. The central concern of this chapter therefore is with what in quantitative terms, and in most cases also in terms of its effectiveness, is one of the least important forms of communication of information about places to their markets. As was stressed in the preceding chapter, most conscious promotion is operating upon an existing information set, reinforcing existing views or endeavouring to correct what is regarded as negative or contradictory information. A second, and equally sobering, thought is that in much place marketing both the consumer and the intended behavioural change are so vaguely defined that many activities included under the title cannot really be defined as promotion using a strict definition of the term.

The simplicity of the definition given above conceals the existence of three problems that complicate the promotion process. Logically the first of these is the *strategic question*, that is, the reason why behaviour is to be influenced, or more broadly the determination of the overall marketing objective. In place marketing in particular the answer is complicated by the absence of the clear market exchange mechanism, present in the case of most commercial products. That is not to argue that all promotion must be intended directly to influence purchasing behaviour: much place promotion, especially by public agencies, is aimed at generating an awareness which only later will be converted into purchase, and this frequently by other agencies. It is also both possible and not uncommon for purchasing to be defined in terms other than merely increased sales or participation. Such aspects of customer behaviour as the time or location of purchase or even the broader community goals of 'social marketing' described in Chapter 2, may be strategic objectives. The important point is that such promotional objectives must be predetermined and defined in terms of changes in the attitudes and behaviour of customers. Many place promotional exercises of public authorities are often reduced to little more than extending a vague awareness of a place, or some broad attribute of it, on the justification that any promotion must be worth something, even if this 'something' remains undefined and immeasurable. This problem is strictly speaking not one of promotion as such, but is inherited from the earlier goal determination phase of the marketing process. However, if the promotional exercise is not viewed in its broader marketing context but becomes detached from the strategic objectives of marketing as a whole, as discussed in Chapter 3, then it has ceased to have much purpose.

Secondly, there is the *information question*, which determines what is to be communicated, and which is in part dependent upon answers to the first question. Finally there is the *tactical* decision of how selected information is to be conveyed most effectively to the potential consumer. Again it needs stressing at the outset that all too often promotion is equated simply with advertising, which is only one possible channel of communication alongside the others described in Chapter 3. A lengthy list of possible promotional methods could be drawn up but would almost certainly be incomplete (see for example Schudson, 1984; Middleton, 1988), but the point being emphasised here is that in the promotion of places, the awareness, interest or favourable image sought may be furthered as much by the discreet lobbying of key decision–makers and opinion leaders as by newspaper advertisements or the indiscriminate distribution of coloured pamphlets. Unfortunately for our purposes, whereas advertising is public and monitorable, many of the other forms of promotion, especially public relations, are either so indirect or even clandestine, as to be all but impossible to research. It must be remembered therefore that the choice of instruments described in many of the cases of place promotion discussed here reflects the ease of collecting information as much as their actual relative importance within place promotion.

The general relations of mental images and individual behaviour was sketched in Chapter 6 and the particular aspect of this wide field of behavioural psychology of interest here is the possibility of influencing the attitude, and thus consequently the behaviour, of an individual towards a place. The problem is not merely one of supplying information. The schemata or structures by means of which information is appraised, as discussed in the previous chapter, are not immutable but are constantly tested for reliability against experience and altered accordingly. The task here then is to induce such modification or elaboration so that a place-image is formed that is receptive to the idea of 'buying' the city.

The origins of marketing in the commercial sector account for the stress on 'purchasing' as the intended behavioural change, but equally other aspects of the behaviour of the individual consumer could be substituted as appropriate. Figure 7.1 shows a simple path through purchasing behaviour, from the recognition of an existing problem or need by a potential purchaser, through the phase of the search for solutions and their evaluation, which is likely of course to be reiterated, to the final purchase decision and resulting action. The obvious point, that will be developed at length later, is that promotion can be used to modify attitudes and thus

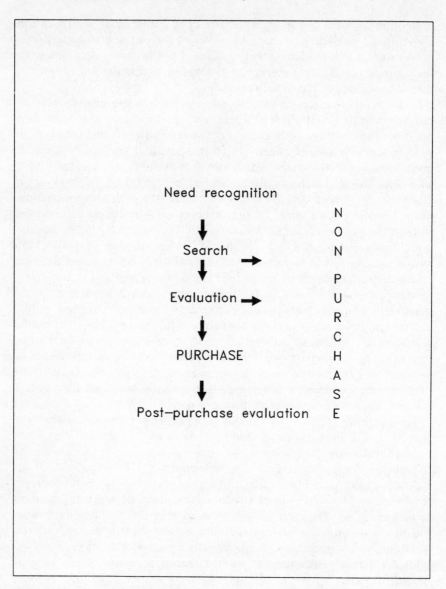

**Figure 7.1**   *A purchase decision-making path*

behaviour during each of the phases outlined, and that a different sort of promotion is likely to be effective at different stages of the path.

## Transmission of place-images

Transmission forms the link between the images held by individuals, as examined in the previous chapter, and those projected by places. It is the aggregate of the various and diverse channels for communicating inform-ation, which may be composed of clearly identifiable publicity media established for this purpose, or a range of personal experiences and perceptions whose source is difficult to identify and whose intent is incidental. However information is transmitted, the medium of communi-cation is not a neutral conduit but is itself selective both in terms of what, and to whom, information is communicated. It can act as a transformer influencing the nature and strength of the message. For our purposes the important question is how is the information which is used by individuals to shape their images of places obtained: this in turn involves not only the discovery and inventorisation of the various media of transmission but also an assessment of the way information acquired through different information channels is evaluated and used.

   Given the quite obvious importance of the answers to these questions in assessing the effectiveness of promotional policies, it is not surprising that investigation into the transmission of information is routinely conducted by many commercial organisations. Most of this research, however, is unpublished, confidential and relates only to the products of particular companies rather than to places as a whole. This is especially unfortunate because it is precisely during this transmission phase in the process that the deliberately projected images are competing for attention with interfering or contrary messages from other sources.

### *Transmission of received place-images*

The primary line of investigation into what are the channels of communi-cation can be pursued from either the side of the recipient or that of the product. Individuals can be asked not only to describe the place-images they hold, as discussed earlier, but also to list the sources of information used to construct such images. This is frequently a routine procedure for monitoring the effectiveness of promotional expenditure, and if not, it should be.

   As might be expected with place marketing, such monitoring of the efficiency of transmission media has been most extensively performed in the tourism industry, although it could equally well be applied to other types of place customer. The procedures are generally simple: those engaged in tourist activities are asked about their use of various official and unofficial sources of information about the area. There are, however, a number of difficulties about interpreting the results of such investigations. If inform-ation is only obtained, as is generally the case, from actual visitors, then only successful transmission is being monitored. Respondents are genuinely and understandably incapable of recognising, let alone assessing, the importance of all sources of information about places: much that is known falls into the category of 'common knowledge' even though there is no agreement about what that constitutes. Finally much of this sort of research produces undifferentiated inventories, the content of which is frequently predetermined by the nature of the questions asked because some information, however trivial, has almost inevitably been obtained from any source included on any such check-list.

Despite these difficulties there exists enough research along these lines to arrive at a general consensus about the main sources of information used. As regards sources for images of tourist destinations (summarised in Crompton, 1979b; and Goodall, 1988) there appear to be three main categories, namely, individual experience, either at first hand or through the personally related experiences of acquaintances; secondly, what might be termed 'professional' information and advice; and thirdly, a type of common knowledge which has been formed from a wide variety of often unacknowledged sources, including public advertising. The first and second are generally readily admitted by consumers as being important, and usually in that order, but the third is frequently underemphasised or even ignored. It is probably genuinely difficult to identify the source of common knowledge and there may be a reluctance to admit to being influenced by generalised place advertising, or even press news reporting, and a bias towards an admitted dependence upon personal sources results.

Most research on the actual use of information sources has concentrated upon the first two categories. The use of tourist information centres as a means of transmitting information to existing committed visitors has been examined in Norwich (Ashworth and de Haan, 1986), where it was revealed that only 16 per cent of visitors actually used this service during their stay but that this modest market penetration increased with length of stay, lack of previous holiday experience in the town and distance travelled. Similar work on the actual use of printed information about tourism destinations has revealed a similar low level of penetration in East Anglia (Ashworth and de Haan, 1986) and the Languedoc coast (Ashworth and de Haan, 1987) and the same range of visitor characteristics was revealed to be affecting these levels as with the TICs. This research has also confirmed that commercial guide books, such as Michelin or Baedeker, or those produced by the motoring organisations in various countries, are used by only a small minority of holiday-makers as an information source during the visit.

These similar findings by different researchers in different locations are discouraging for official promotion agencies, especially as they cast doubt upon the viability of managing tourist behaviour in destinations by means of controlling the nature of the information supplied to visitors. There may be a tendency to fail to admit the use of these professional sources, and it has been suggested (Buck, 1988) that such information has an important indirect importance by influencing intermediaries who themselves are an important influence on customer opinion.

Kok *et al.* (1985) made a similar assessment of the information sources used by potential investors in the Netherlands. A clear distinction emerged between three types of sources of information about places which investors used to shape their 'informational environment'. The most widely used and valued sources were the opinions of existing customers and suppliers; other professionals, including consultants, were less used and valued, while the least important category was public sources of information, including information supplied by local authorities. Despite the possibility of an element of under-representation of the last category, there is the same clear progression as was found in information sources on tourism, from highly valued personal sources to lower valued public sources. The implications for public sector city marketing are sobering and considered later in this chapter.

*Transmission of projected place-images*

The transmission of place-images can equally be investigated from the side of their projection. In the case of deliberately promoted images designed to affect consumer behaviour this is in practice a study of the composition of the marketing mix as described in Chapter 3 as an integral part of the market planning procedure. At its simplest level this involves studies such as that of Bartels and Timmer (1987) which sampled local authorities in the Netherlands with the objective, amongst others, of discovering which media were used for place promotion. In the 160 authorities admitting to such exercises during the period 1980–87, almost a third of all expenditure was devoted to generalised advertising in the public media, designed to create a favourable image of the authority among an undifferentiated public. Promotion through transmission channels more carefully directed at already interested customers, such as informational brochures and exhibitions accounted for smaller proportions of the budget; the remainder was largely accounted for by public relations operations which, it can be assumed, are the most carefully targeted.

Although it is difficult to make direct comparisons between research findings, if only because the definitions of the different components within the marketing mix vary, it is probable that much the same broad division of promotional effort between channels will be found elsewhere. Burgess (1982), for example, examined the chosen marketing mix of British local authorities in the late 1970s and discovered a similar spectrum of communication channels ranging from weakly targeted public media advertising, through more directed exhibitions and promotion to enquirers and other identified potential users, to closely targeted public relations

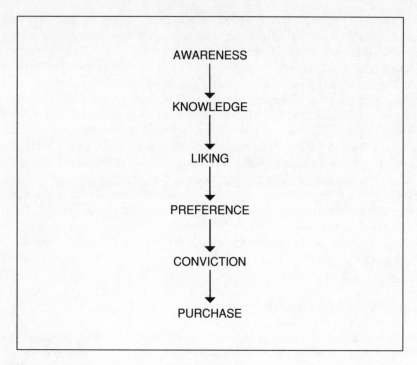

**Figure 7.2**   *Cognitive stages in purchase behaviour*

exercises aimed at specific firms, decision-makers, and intermediaries. A major difficulty of assessing the use of various channels of communication by promoters is that activities at one end of this spectrum, being by definition in the public domain, are both more intrusive and accessible to the researchers than activities at the other, where public relations merges into private lobbying. The danger therefore is that almost all academic research has concentrated upon only one set of promotional instruments (the last in the well–known triad of promotional techniques, 'booze, boosterism and brochures') and conclusions about media selection in the promotional effort as a whole can only be tentative.

This perhaps matters less if it is accepted that different marketing mixes tend to be used at different stages in the complex process of the consumer's decision to use the facilities offered by a place. The range of mental states of the potential place user during the purchase decision process can be summarised as in Figure 7.2. Van Raaij (1986) has complicated this idea by suggesting that what in fact occurs is not a single linear decision-making process leading to purchase but a related set of separate processes, including the decision to be interested generically in the subject, specific purchase-directed behaviour, and then a process of reflection and evaluation. Thus the resulting action could as well be re-purchase or complaint as purchase. The important point here is that the 'cone of decision-making' discussed in the previous chapter in terms of opportunity sets can be related to this progression through states of mind. These in turn can be modified by the 'spectrum' of promotional media suggested above with the intention of sensitising, persuading, heightening the appreciation, or justifying as appropriate (van Raaij, 1984). Public media advertising is most effective in influencing large numbers at the early broad exploration stages, while the more directed media and public relations are brought into play for transmitting specific information and characteristics of places to a more restricted market at the narrower end of the 'cone'.

The various cognitive processes undergone by the potential purchaser at different stages of this decision–making have been described in a number of different 'readiness to buy' models. Some of these are arrayed in Table 7.1 against various types of promotion that are likely to be particularly appropriate at that phase.

Thus most research, by concentrating upon the more publicly available media, is in fact investigating the early decisions about places. In the choice of holiday destination, for example, in which some fragmentary information exists about the effects of lobbying upon the influential intermediaries that market particular holiday packages to individual consumers, it has been argued (Buck, 1988) that public advertising is effective in establishing the style of holiday preferred and its general national or regional location, but that the particular place and package purchased is strongly influenced by the information and opinions of professional intermediaries conveyed through personal 'lobbying'.

There is a quite fundamental question of the different spatial distribution of supply and demand that is inherent in the promotion of places to outsiders, whether potential tourists, residents or investors. The product is concentrated in space but the market is not. The initial place promotion exercise therefore has to be directed at a widely dispersed market in which potential customers are heavily diluted by non-customers. The future

**Table 7.1** Readiness to buy models and appropriate promotion

|  | AIDA models | Hierarchy of effects model | Adoption model | Media |
| --- | --- | --- | --- | --- |
| Cognitive | Attention | Awareness/ knowledge | Awareness | Publicity |
|  |  |  |  | Education |
| Affective desire | Intent/ preference | Liking/ evaluation | Internal | Advertising |
| Behavioural | Action | Purchase | Trial/ adoption | Personal Selling |

residents in a particular new town, commercial entrepreneurs in a specific industrial estate or holiday-makers to a named resort, will form a minute proportion of any international or even national population. Therefore promotion at this stage is most likely to be highly generalised mass media advertising at a low cost per recipient. The higher cost, and more closely targeted media used to convey more detailed information about the characteristics of places will be reserved for customers who have been identified, or more usually identified themselves by their information search behaviour.

Many different information media used in this public phase of the promotional exercise have been investigated. These include public press advertising at various spatial scales (see Pocock and Hudson, 1978), or specifically of British new towns (Goodey, 1974), or such slogan advertising as on postmarks or car bumper stickers propagating the names and nicknames of states and cities in the United States (Kane and Alexander, 1965) or more recently France (Montalieu, 1988). The content of non-advertising media of widely varying types has also been investigated, such as film (Gold, 1985), television (Gould and Lyew–Ayee, 1985), news reporting (Goodey, 1968; Brooker-Gross, 1985), popular music (Jarvis, 1985) and even gossip (Burgess, 1985).

If much of the Anglo-American work has been focused on the popular media, much French work has concentrated on the use of public art works as a means of deliberately shaping a public awareness of place identities. Encouraged by the central government (Bavoux and Paget, 1986; Coste, 1989), various local authorities have set about creating a civic self-consciousness through the sponsorship of publicly accessible physical works of art and civic design (Bavoux, 1989), and have claimed dramatic results. For example, the economically depressed suburb of Oullins on the edge of the Lyon Agglomeration was perceived as lacking a separate identity by both residents and others. However, a local authority campaign under the slogan 'create a city' included the use of street art with the result that in a survey in 1989, three-quarters of the population recognized it as a distinct urban entity (Gault, 1989).

The most common analysis, however, has been performed upon printed promotional information originating from the marketing departments of local authorities and distributed in response to potential customer enquiries. These channels of information have produced the materials that form the bulk of the analysis of place–images for potential investors in the North Netherlands (van der Veen and Voogd, 1987; Voogd and van der Wijk, 1989), and for recreational visitors in Languedoc (Ashworth and de Haan, 1987) discussed later. Burgess's (1982) analysis of British local authorities' images has even subdivided this sort of promotional package into 'town guides' used for very broad undifferentiated markets, 'glossy brochures' for general commercial enquirers, 'fact sheets' for more specific 'hard sell' commercial information, and 'tourist guides', used principally for influencing the customer behaviour of existing visitors. Attempts to relate in more detail these particular media of transmission with particular markets or particular image characteristics tends to be unprofitable, if only because the experience of all three of the studies referred to above suggests that local authorities themselves tend not to make such fine distinctions and generally swamp enquirers with the total package of printed information, leaving the selection of relevant information from these to the potential customer.

*Credibility of transmission channels*

In order to be effective information must not only be transmitted along the appropriate communication channels to reach potential customers so as to be actually received by them; it must also be accepted. Most of the information that continually bombards individuals is ignored or rejected. If a piece of information is to be incorporated into the cognitive image of a place, it must be credible: in Uzzell's (1984) terms 'active collusion' is needed. Much of the credibility stems from the user's evaluation of the medium of transmission as much as the character of the information itself. This credibility, according to Burgess (1982), is dependent upon both factors related to the source of the information and also to the style of presentation of the information. How information is transmitted will therefore be as important as what is transmitted in establishing the acceptability of the message to the recipient.

The difference between the use of an information source and the value placed upon the information it conveyed was examined by Crompton (1979a), whose respondents produced significantly different rank orders of sources when asked to list both sources used and sources relied upon for information about holiday destinations. Nolan (1976) investigated this credibility for various tourist marketing media in terms of the recipient's confidence in the accuracy, objectivity, informational content and personal involvement. Official printed information and counter services were seen as the most credible, while press and broadcasting advertising were regarded as the least believable. He also concluded that most recipients claimed to recognise and discount promotional bias and hyperbole, and rate highly what they regarded as sources of useful factual information. Both the World Tourism Organisation (WTO, 1985) and Crompton (1979a) confirm that 'official' information, namely that endorsed by national or local official agencies, including local authorities, is rated as more 'authentic', and thus more likely to be accepted than that produced by commercial firms.

Gitelson and Crompton (1983) drew a distinction between non-personal destination specific literature, which is regarded as informative, and the personal opinions and advice of friends, professional advisers and also first-hand experience, which has an evaluative or legitimising function. This distinction can be applied to the stages of decision–making, to return to Goodall's model (see Figure 6.1.), which could in this context apply equally to users other than recreational visitors. Sources regarded as authentic and accurate as well as those that are factually informative, even if recognisably biased, will be highly valued in the initial stages of selecting destinations. The information packets issued by development authorities and departments, such as those examined by van der Veen and Voogd (1987), and by tourist boards (Pattinson, 1990), would fall into this category. However, the final decision will require legitimising by a more personal source, whether at first hand through an exploratory site visit, or if this is not feasible as with many tourist decisions, through personal contacts whether acquaintances or professional intermediaries. This stage is less a search for further information, although it may be publicly presented as such, than for legitimising information already obtained in earlier phases through other sources. In the selling of tourism destinations, the travel agent, and in the attraction of investors, the public relations agent or investment consultant, clearly have an important function at this stage. These communication channels tend to be underestimated in much of the research into place–images already described, if only because being interpersonal contacts they are difficult to describe objectively.

## Place-image promotion and decision-making

Many of the difficulties of analysing the various sorts of received and transmitted place-images discussed above also occur in the study of projected images. Consequently studies of such images have concentrated principally upon promotional images, that is those that are deliberately promoted to an envisaged market with the intention of altering consumer attitudes and thus behaviour. The large financial resources devoted to promotion by private and public organisations has provided a potent incentive for these to monitor the effectiveness of their own output and alter its content accordingly.

What in the marketing of a physical product is termed 'brand recognition' has a counterpart in place marketing as the association of potential users of a place with its promoted attributes. The amount of success achieved in this respect in relation to the resources devoted to it needs continuous monitoring. The complaint that this is not performed adequately, or at all, by many organisations engaged in place marketing in particular (Walker, 1976; Burgess, 1982; Burgess and Gold, 1985) does not detract from the fact that such 'market research' has generated an enormous quantity of useful information on the characteristics of place-images, whether these were successfully promoted or not. Unfortunately such information has a definite monetary value to the organisation and its competitors and access to it is understandably restricted which makes comparative research very difficult. Therefore the research reviewed here represents only that fraction of investigations into promoted images that are open to public scrutiny.

There is, however, another line of investigation into projected place-images which is concerned with images that are not deliberately promoted, in the sense defined above, but were projected as a by-product of some other objective. The relevance of these studies to promoted images is clearly that they outline the context and the competition within which promoted place–images operate. From our viewpoint the projection of this stream of unofficial and generally uncontrolled information represents at best 'noise' and 'interference' interrupting, concealing and distorting the transmission, and at worst it competes by presenting contradictory or distractingly irrelevant information.

Fortunately many aspects of this important context have been reviewed by researchers interested in the elements of place-images contained in culture, broadly defined. Here, as opposed to the deliberate use of public art discussed earlier, the effect upon urban images is incidental and unintended, but no less powerful for that. An extensive body of research exists on the evocative effects of literature, music and fine art on the shaping of the images of places, much of which is summarised by Pocock (1981). Similarly the amount and type of coverage allocated by the public press and broadcasting media to particular places and the resulting effects upon the way places are regarded has been the subject of the large number of very varied studies brought together in Burgess and Gold (1985). In more detail Burgess and Wood (1988) have examined such coverage of the London Docklands area, comparing these presentations and the ideas suggested by them with the goals of the development authority.

These lines of investigation, however important in describing the context within which promoted images operate, are concerned with making some sense of the enormous quantity of vaguely directed information that has ill-defined and usually unintended effects upon the way places are viewed. Promoted images, on the other hand, although forming a much smaller proportion of the quantity of messages in circulation, should be relatively more effective, by virtue of them being both more clearly drawn and directed.

*Dilemmas in place promotion*

Before considering in more detail case studies of such research as is available into the content of particular promoted place-images, some general comparative elements in place-images can be considered. An organisation contemplating place promotion and having, consciously or not, proceeded through the earlier stages of market planning as described in Chapter 3, faces a number of fundamental questions about how to promote the chosen place attributes. Thus it is assumed by this stage that the decision about product definition tackled in Chapter 5, and those of market targeting in Chapter 4, have been made. The following promotional problem can be most easily approached through the consideration of a series of dilemmas.

The first of these can be labelled the *information/persuasion dilemma* as the choice is made as to how much information about the place should be conveyed in the message being promoted. To take an extreme contrast, for example, a postal enquiry to a local authority could be answered by either the 'town guide', a lengthy compendium of useful addresses, lists of facilities, and basic factual information on such possibly useful and varied topics as early closing days, library opening hours and the frequency of bus services, or at the opposite extreme, by a 'glossy', an eye-catching multi-colour pamphlet composed of evocative illustrations and accompanying textual slogans. The first provides possibly essential information with the accuracy of a shotgun but does little either to capture the attention of a recipient considering many alternative places, or endow the place with a distinctive profile in comparison with others. The second approach simplifies the message so as to leave the reader with at least a few simple impressions of the nature of the place at the cost of providing factual information. The same sorts of choices along such a spectrum apply to other vehicles of promotion although the nature of the message may in practice be determined by the constraints of the communication medium itself, so that the question of what to say is in practice resolved into the question of through what medium to say it. Slogan opportunities, for instance, on postmarks, bumper stickers or town notice-boards lend themselves to an extremely simple message of the 'sunshine resort' variety rather then a comprehensive table of climatic data.

The choice depends of course on the purpose of the promotion and the appropriateness of the message to the phase of decision-making reached by the recipient. Slogans, and indeed much general advertising, are using simplicity to convey as directly as possible an uncomplicated impression of usually a single place attribute. The conflict is between effectiveness of communication, which demands compression, and the filtering out of distinctiveness which results from such terseness. At one extreme, slogans of the 'Norwich – a fine city', or 'This year it's got to be India' variety cannot be faulted on the first count but no characteristic of these particular places relevant to any particular group of potential users has survived the compression. At this end of the spectrum the aim of the promotion is no more ambitious than to assert the existence of the town or country which might otherwise have remained unconsidered by an undifferentiated potential market.

Effective promotion will attempt to move along this spectrum in parallel with the potential user's changing requirements for information at the different stages of decision-making. The simple but effective assertion of existence, appropriate at an early stage, shifts through a more distinctive profiling of selected attributes of the places as alternatives are being considered, to the provision of more detailed and relevant information as the final locational selection is being made. The frustration of the business executive whose specific question is answered by a 'glossy', or the casual tourism enquiry, which is answered with a thick town guide, results from a failure of promotion to match the content of the image being projected with the stage of decision-making in the particular market being reached. There are reasons to suggest that place promotion is particularly prone to such errors in image content. This is not only because of the multifaceted nature of the product and its simultaneous use for many different purposes, but also because most of the public authorities conducting such promotion have limited resources, of both money and expertise, for a thorough enough monitoring of the consumer. Even if such information was known, the range of promotional instruments available is usually far too limited; one or two brochures may be all that is available to meet the needs of not merely widely different potential users, but potential customers at quite different stages in the place selection process.

A second, and closely related, dilemma is that between *honesty*, in the sense of striving for accuracy, on the one side, and *hyperbole* on the other. The existence of bias, in the selection and presentation of information to attain particular goals, is not in question, but is inherent in the purposes of competitive promotion: the concern here is the relationship of the content of the message with the actual nature and facilities of the place. A degree of exaggeration of the favourable attributes of the place, and a tendency to underemphasise less attractive attributes, is not only discounted by recipients, but probably expected, and a promotional message that admitted that a particular place was much like many others and had nothing in particular to recommend it, might capture some transient attention by its novelty, but would be unlikely to be effective over more than the very short term. Conversely a message whose hyperbole is so far-fetched as to make claims for a uniqueness that the reality of the place cannot possibly hope to approach, runs the risk of being not credible and, if believed, not sustainable in the user's subsequent experiences, which leads inevitably to customer dissatisfaction. The high level of post-holiday complaints in some sections of the tourism industry (see Dann, 1978; Buck, 1988) stems in part from an over-wide gap between the expectations evoked by promotion and the reality of the holiday; the particular dependence of customer choice on promotional material without the corrective of first-hand experience, together with the particularly fierce competition between a large number of places, each offering very similar holidays, lends itself to such problems.

The third dilemma about message content recognises the context of promotion within the much wider communication of place-images and is an admission of the modest influence that such directed promotion can have upon consumers in competition with other projected images. Schmoll

(1977, p. 54) saw the role of promotion as, 'rather more to reinforce existing desirable images than to correct or to neutralise negative image elements'. The *strengths/weaknesses dilemma* stems from this admission. A concentration upon strengths is upon those place attributes which favour the objectives of the promotion and are already established in the image held by the consumers. This is clearly an attractive strategy, as the recipient is predisposed to accept the message although if the idea is already firmly established, its promotion becomes unnecessary. Conversely the alternative, the weakness strategy, is necessary but technically difficult. A promotional message intended to counter an existing negative image runs the risk of inadvertently propagating that image. The recent tourism campaigns advertising that the United States was not expensive, Parisians were not brusque, and English seaside resorts not frequently rained upon, probably reinforced the contrary message and certainly brought these unattractive attributes to the attention of any consumer not yet aware of them. The chosen 1990 slogan for the city of Groningen (NL), whose principal image weakness in attracting commercial investment from outside is its perceived national peripherality, is 'there's nothing above Groningen'. This could be regarded as a clever exploitation of an existing well–established negative attribute, or a particularly inept advertising of a major drawback that would have been better underplayed. The choice between the easy but possibly unnecessary promotion of strengths and the difficult but necessary countering of weaknesses is in practice resolved by adopting strategies along the spectrum between these extremes. Existing favourable images provide the initial acceptability for a message designed to build upon such attributes and it is hoped enlarge and extend them to cover or compensate for the existing weaknesses.

A common aspect of this problem is not so much the defensive use of messages to counter weakness, as the devising of a strategy capable of handling the consequences of an image so strong as to preclude any attempt to alter it and thus to alter the nature of the place-product, however desirable that might be to the place concerned. Examples of this phenomenon can be found at various spatial scales and for various markets. There are many instances of tourist places which possess such a well-established popular image that attempts to broaden or alter the market appeal, in terms of type of holiday or use of space, is very difficult. The seaside resorts of the Spanish Mediterranean coast, for example, (Barke and France, 1986) have attempted both to move the product up-market and to include the inland historic towns in the itinerary of visitors but have found it extremely difficult to broaden the highly successful image of the existing beach resort holiday, successfully promoted over the last 20 years. Even within a single city the same spatial–promotional dilemma can be found. In Norwich (UK), as in many such tourist-historic cities, the problem can be simply stated as which part of the city should be promoted. The city's success in promoting itself as an historic city has established a small area of the central city, containing a small group of historic monuments, firmly in the imagination of visitors as the 'Norwich experience'. If the goal of the city authorities is to maximise the number of visitors, then promotion should capitalise upon existing success by reinforcing expectations. However, if the goal is to spread the benefits of tourism through a wider part of the city, and thus also to reduce the costs of congestion in the existing tourist concentrations, then promotion should concentrate upon new historic attractions and areas which are not yet established in the image of potential visitors. This second policy has in fact been attempted (Berkers *et al.*, 1986) but diverting the flow of information projected to visitors on alternative areas risks losing visitors to competing cities.

Not only may it be difficult to alter a firmly established image for a particular group of users, it may also prove difficult to promote a place to a potential market if its image has already been successfully promoted to a quite different market. Burgess (1982) has described many logical inconsistencies in British local authority promotion, such as the simultaneous promotion of dynamism and heritage, or unspoilt landscape and development possibilities. In practice such logical incongruities may be overlooked. The existence and seriousness of such a problem depends upon the nature of the various place attributes promoted and the degree of segregation of the different markets. Curious juxtapositions of image can exist, as Great Yarmouth (beach resort and North Sea supply base) or Cambridge (historic city and electronics centre); but these depend upon non-contradictory images or promotion that is along such separate channels of transmission as not to interfere with each other.

*Some cases*

The operation of these general dilemmas, and the compromise solutions adopted, can now be examined in the content of some detailed cases.

*The North Netherlands Experiment*   This was a set of related research projects into promoted place-images undertaken for a mixture of academic and practical planning purposes in a number of locations in the northern part of the Netherlands. The term 'experiment' is applicable because information was collected under elaborately constructed experimental conditions so that the promotional messages obtained had been targeted as closely as possible to a potential private sector commercial investor. The Northern Netherlands was selected because it has suffered from a long-term relative economic decline in its staple industries, and has for some years been in search of new economic activities, and consequently most local authorities in the area pursue active acquisition policies of one sort or another.

**Table 7.2**   Elements in the promotional image of local authorities in the Northern Netherlands

|  | % of local authorities |
|---|---|
| History | |
| Description of Historic Buildings | 56 |
| Historic walk | 56 |
| List of museums | 50 |
| Account of history | 44 |
| Description of coat of arms | 31 |
| List of conserved buildings | 25 |
| Recreation | |
| Tourist office brochure | 69 |
| Water recreation facilities | 38 |
| Sport facilities | 31 |
| Description of cafes/restaurants | 25 |
| List of events | 19 |
| Parks/open spaces | 6 |
| Other facilities | |
| Parking | 31 |
| Local authority services | 31 |
| Housing | 6 |
| Schools | 6 |
| General | |
| Account of district | 81 |
| Town guide | 50 |
| Town map | 50 |

[After Voogd and van der Wijk 1989]

The objective of one piece of the research (reported in van der Veen and Voogd, 1989) was to obtain and describe the elements composing the place-image as promoted by local authorities in response to enquiry from this potential market. Seventy-eight local authorities ('gemeenten') supplied information under the experimental conditions and the content of the resulting local images is described in Table 7.2.

The most notable general characteristic is the dependence of those images upon three elements. First, although surprisingly, given the targeted market, quantitatively the least significant of the three was the attempt to portray a favourable 'entrepreneurial climate' pervading the authority. This was attempted by means of relating past successful economic activities, current commercial activities, the extent of land availability and cheapness, a co-operative local authority administrative apparatus and an industrious local workforce. This last was often portrayed by recourse to a romantic historicism extolling the relevant racial and ethnic virtues of the populace. Secondly, there was a more or less factual description, usually supported by statistical material, of the cultural, educational, recreational and housing infrastructure in terms of actual facilities. Thirdly, and quantitatively the most important, was the attempt to project the two attributes of landscape beauty, with its implied concomitants of peace and tranquillity, and historicity, implying stability and continuity. This was achieved by describing the place as being steeped in historical experiences and possessing numerous surviving conserved artefacts from these experiences.

These three dominant elements in the Northern Netherlands can be compared with those described by Burgess (1982) in the United Kingdom. She identified four general attributes of the place being promoted, namely centrality, dynamism, identity, quality of life. But the last two were in practice dependent upon the elements of landscape beauty, historicity, cultural and social facilities as found in the Dutch case.

This promotion of an image mainly composed of elements of broad-based 'amenity', whether of the natural and historic built environment or residential and social facilities, needs explanation, especially when it is recalled that this information was elicited in response to an enquiry from a potential commercial investor, not from potential recreational visitors or residents. Given the ubiquity, at least in this region, of the attributes selected for promotion, almost all authorities were projecting substantially the same image, although they were aware that within this experiment they were in a competitive situation. Nor was there a significant difference in this respect between the larger authorities, who might be expected to have a wider range of publicity materials at their disposal and to employ specialist departments of assigned individuals to process them, and the smaller ones, who were more likely to be compelled to use multipurpose information.

There was similarly near unanimity in the choice of projectional media, with the glossy pamphlet predominating, supported on occasion by extracts from reports or statistical digests, and there was little attempt to follow up the initial contacts with other and more personal promotion. In short, although 'the single most important locational factor is the nature and quality of information on the areas concerned' (Burgess, 1982, p. 2), and it might be expected that the local authority would be a major source of such information, nevertheless in practice a weakly profiled product was being promoted through limited channels to an undifferentiated market. There is unfortunately little reason to suspect that the Northern Netherlands is untypical of many such regions in this respect.

*History as an element in the promoted image of Dutch towns* The questions thus raised about the content of public sector promoted place-

**Table 7.3** Elements in the promotional image of 16 medium sized Dutch towns

| Types of information | % of towns |
| --- | --- |
| General overview | 81 |
| Tourist overview | 69 |
| Description of monuments | 56 |
| Historical town trail | 56 |
| Description of museums | 50 |
| Town guide | 50 |
| Town map | 50 |
| Historical account | 44 |
| Water recreation facilities | 31 |
| Description of coat of arms | 31 |
| Sport facilities | 31 |
| Parking facilities | 31 |
| Other public services | 31 |
| Lists of monuments | 25 |
| Lists of cafes/restaurants | 25 |
| Calender of events | 19 |
| List of commercial firms | 19 |
| Description of public parks | 6 |
| Description of housing | 6 |
| Description of schools | 6 |

images were pursued in a similarly constructed study concentrating on 16 medium-sized urban authorities drawn from a country-wide sample. The objective was to examine quite specifically the role of the most important 'amenity' element, namely history, contained in the images promoted by local authorities to potential investors. The results (reported in full in Voogd and van de Wijk, 1989) first describe the quantitative importance of this element (Table 7.3) and secondly, the proportion of historical attributes, as well as other elements, such as business affairs, infrastructural facilities, and residential amenity, in the promoted image as a whole (Figure 7.3). Despite considerable variation in the structure of images from town to town, the overwhelmingly dominant pattern is clear: historical attributes are being widely used to shape distinctive urban images targeted to potential exogenous commercial investors. Historicity, in its various forms, had an almost monopolistic dominance in four of the towns, in four more it was the most important element and in only five did it play no appreciable role. The strength of this element does not seem to be related to either the existing monumental endowment of cities, their existing established images for other purposes, such as historic city tourism, nor the size or viability of their existing commercial sectors.

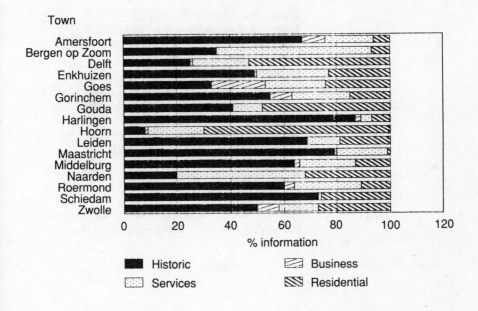

**Figure 7.3**  *The significance of historical and other elements in promotional images in medium-sized Dutch towns*

*Promoted images of Languedoc*  The Languedoc study was concerned with a different market and concentrated upon promoted holiday destination images in 11 separate resorts on the Mediterranean coast of southwest France. It was attempting to trace the whole process of place-image promotion from projection to reception and simultaneously relate it to both product characteristics and consumer behaviour (see Ashworth and de Haan, 1987).

One of the most significant conclusions was that the images promoted to existing visitors by the tourism authorities in the individual resorts did not differ essentially from each other, all resorts being presented as dominantly outdoor activity centres, offering a range of sporting possibilities on broad sandy beaches, associated water surfaces and harbour areas under a bright Mediterranean sun (Figure 7.4). This clear-cut promoted image raises three problems. First, the attributes of the promoted image largely ignore the climatic, site and other deficiencies of the coast as a whole. Secondly,

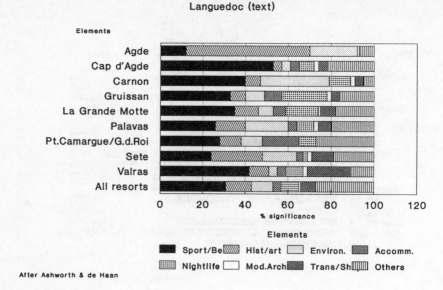

**Figure 7.4**   *Elements in the promoted images of Languedoc resorts*

and more significantly, they largely ignore the variations in resource endowment between the individual resorts. More or less the same image is being presented for resorts offering quite different holiday packages, often to substantially different markets, in terms of such characteristics of visitors as their length of stay, choice of type of accommodation, country of origin and previous holiday experience. Thirdly, the visitors to the coast had a dominant image of the resorts as pleasant, peaceful, unpretentious places and their pattern of holiday behaviour, dividing their time between beach and café, largely reflected this image.

Explanations of these discrepancies were sought in the choice of marketing strategies and in the problem of selecting an appropriate spatial scale. The first is a variant of the strengths/weaknesses dilemma. Most visitors to most of these resorts were either resident in the region or French nationals with a high rate of return to the same resort. It was these visitors who largely shaped the received image of peace and pleasant tranquillity, and whose largely passive behaviour patterns were dominant. These loyal and locally knowledgeable visitors were not particularly receptive to promotion. The promotion exercises of the local agencies were aimed at the less experienced, possibly foreign and certainly non-local, new markets. They were therefore 'aggressive' rather than 'defensive', projecting an image of active, boat-associated, sportive holidays that accorded well with a widely-held general image of a Mediterranean holiday rather than reflecting either the actual facilities of the resorts or the actual behaviour of most existing holiday–makers.

Secondly, there is the problem of appropriate spatial scale for promotion. As argued in Chapter 5, places, unlike most products, exist within a nesting hierarchy of spatial scales. In this instance the choice had been made by the local tourism agencies to focus promotion upon the level of the intermediate resort region, which accounts for the lack of much variation between the projected images of the individual resorts. In addition the concentration upon shaping a destination image of the Languedoc coast as a region offering more or less indistinguishable beach and water associated activity centres, backed by a hinterland of interesting natural landscapes and small historic towns, creates two discrepancies. One with the place-images held by visitors, which did distinguish individual resort characteristics to a considerable degree, and another with the spatial behaviour of those visitors, which to a large extent ignored possible attractions, whether in the rural hinterland or other coastal places, outside the chosen resort.

A major complication in selecting the spatial scale to be promoted is that the visitors to the Languedoc coast did not form a homogeneous market. Different groups held place–images focusing on different spatial scales. In particular visitors from within the region itself, or those with a long–standing familiarity with the holiday possibilities on the coast, formed a majority of the holiday-makers. These local *habitués* held a relatively clear image of their particular resorts but largely projected this resort image unaltered on to the wider scale. In other words, they had no clear image of the region other than as an extension of the resort, even though its actual attributes were quite different. Visitors from further away, and those with little or no previous experience, tended to reverse the process of identification; namely they had an image of Languedoc, or even the Mediterranean coast in general, mostly derived from other than first-hand experience, to which their image of individual resorts concurred as a sort of microcosm of the wider scale. Understandably these visitors also used the resources of the wider region more intensively through their excursion behaviour. The promoted images tended to reinforce those already held by this second group. Conversely they tended to conflict with that held by the first group, which mattered less because it was this group that was, in any event, less receptive to publicity information.

*Promoted images and planning goals*

The dilemmas outlined above and their applications in a brief description of a few case studies, serves to reiterate an important axiom. The success of the promotion of place–images cannot be assessed only in terms of intrinsic authenticity (i.e. its concordance with the actual characteristics and facilities of the place), its effectiveness (i.e. its consequences in customer behaviour) nor congruence between the promoted and received images. Place–images are promoted by organisations concerned with achieving particular management goals in the area concerned and success must be measured against such predetermined goals. Place-image promotion should be seen as one planning instrument within the market planning process as a whole, and used in preference to or in combination with other non-market–oriented place management techniques.

In the cases examined above, for example, the place images of the Northern Netherlands or of Languedoc were promoted by public authorities, or by private agencies with public responsibilities, as part of long-standing regional planning policies. These broader planning policies in turn determined the overall goals of the promotional operation which in both cases was only indirectly to increase product sales in conventional marketing terms. Increased private commercial investment in the one case, and the attraction of more, or higher spending, tourists in the other, were only means of achieving the economic objectives of the regional planners, not ends in themselves.

This is an obvious but necessary disclaimer and its neglect lies behind a number of the discrepancies and problems discussed above. The problem simply stated is which image should be promoted in furtherance of which goal.

The distinctive characteristics of places as marketable products, as described in Chapter 5, are inevitably reflected in the manner and content of their promotion. Places are an aggregation of many multifunctional facilities and attributes, some of which are highly specific, clearly recognisable and easily measurable, while others are vague and diffuse qualities. In addition, various combinations of such attributes are simultaneously in use by quite different groups of consumers for quite different purposes. The number and variety of possible images is thus enormous and a wide variety of promotional images may be necessary, while an equally wide variety of projected images from other sources is likely to exist. It is this that both provides wide promotional opportunities but also accounts for the dilemmas related above.

There is a further set of equally inherent difficulties related to the product which can be termed, the *place-image delimitation problem*. Unlike many other products on the market, places are intrinsically difficult to delimit. Their boundaries are unclear in two separate senses. The images of particular places are imprecisely located in space so that they either overlap, or underlap, leaving mental black holes in the field of consciousness of potential users. They also exist within scale hierarchies, so that one place is a constituent part of a number of nesting regions, each of which is itself vaguely delimited in relation to other levels in such a hierarchy. These characteristics have a number of consequences for place-image promotion. The problem of spatial scale selection within such a hierarchy was referred to in the Languedoc case, but there are more

*Image building and the promotion of places*    123

extreme examples where conflict occurs between images at different levels. This encourages promotion to be highly selective. The tourism industry is notorious for propagating its own mental geography, by concentrating on promoting the level with the most favourable existing image and ignoring levels with unfavourable images; by creating entirely new regions (such as 'the Cornish Riviera', 'the Shakespeare Country' and the like); as well as stretching existing regional designations if their image is favourable or contracting them if not (see the many examples given in Goodall, 1988).

A further problem is the shadow effect, namely that the image of one place is likely to overshadow the image of neighbouring places, even if these are intrinsically quite different. Such shadowing may be positive, as a place reaps the benefits of the attractive image and promotional efforts of its neighbour, or negative where a place suffers through spatial association with the poor image of its neighbour. The lesson is that the promotion of one place must take account of the promotion of others, which it will in turn affect, depending upon the structure of the mental geography of customers. The promotional efforts of the large number of mainly small local authorities described above in the 'North Netherlands Experiment', for example, were shadowing each other, leaving an overall regional impression from which they were all benefiting, including non-participating authorities. Promoters will attempt to benefit from favourable shadows by locating their place-product under them, while distancing themselves from unfavourable shadows, even at the cost of considerable distortion of spatial reality. Such techniques are part of the conventional stock–in–trade of tourism promotion in particular, mainly because the potential consumer is likely to have a particularly vague grasp of the geography of the destinations concerned, but is equally detectable in promotion for other markets (for example, the use of place designations by real estate promoters).

These intrinsic characteristics of places as spatial entities, are thus critical influences upon the place-images held by customers and the effectiveness of place promotion in affecting these images. However, place promotion by public authorities is in practice constrained by the actual jurisdictional bounding of the areas for which they are responsible, and there is no guarantee that such boundaries will correspond to those held by users. A local authority area may include regions within it with quite distinct and even conflicting user images. The dilemma then is that a concentration on the regions with the most attractive existing images maximises promotional effectiveness, but may not correspond to the authorities' wider objectives and in any event ignores the interests of a portion of the authorities' voters and local tax payers.

## Integration

A central paradox of this, and the preceding, chapter is that in order to analyse the nature of place-images, they have of necessity been disintegrated and separated from their contextual links with the product and the market, while an understanding of their central role in marketing demands a holistic approach. The dilemma that understanding depends upon integration but analysis upon isolation of the distinct components is not easily resolved. Place-images need to be appreciated within two sorts of integrating frameworks. First, the complete process of creation, transmission and reception needs to be studied as a continuous and circular relationship, yet there are understandable practical reasons why this rarely occurs. It is clear from the various cases discussed above that in terms of research design the sorts of techniques usable for gathering information on the various stages of this process are quite different. The ideal situation would be to collect comparable information upon the image promoted, transmitted and received of the same place, by the same group of users, for the same set of uses. None of the cases presented, or referred to, in this chapter achieve such an ideal. Consequently there are always discontinuities in the tracing of the critical relationships between the different stages in the process. This in turn has serious consequences for our central concern with place promotion, as although different promoted images of one or many places can be analysed and compared with each other at either the production or consumption end of the process, comparison between different stages remains extremely difficult, and it is precisely these comparisons that may determine the efficiency of the promotion exercise.

A second and even broader requirement for an integrated approach is the necessity for relating the complete image promotion process to the targeted consumer on the demand side (Chapter 4) and the product on the supply side (Chapter 5). Images held by consumers result in modifications to actual behaviour in and towards the actual places concerned; similarly images are ultimately derived directly or indirectly from the characteristics, facilities and measurable attributes of the places to which they refer. Therefore again a holistic approach that compares images with the objective realities of places and how they are used is required. The dangers of a distintegrated approach, in which promotional images lose contact with the nature of the product being promoted or where the promotional exercise cannot be related to its effects upon the use of the place concerned, are obvious. The sobering realisation of a number of tourism studies that a high degree of post-purchase customer dissatisfaction exists (Buck, 1988), can frequently be related to the size of the discrepancy between promoted image and the reality of tourism destinations. The weakness of the feedback links between customer behaviour and promoted images contributes towards the notorious instability of the tourism market. But again however desirable, this is extremely difficult to achieve, as can be demonstrated in the cases discussed above.

This is not to deny the validity of the theoretical models suggested in this and the previous chapter, nor the contribution that partial studies have made to understanding these processes as a whole, but only to suggest that studies that focus their attention specifically upon such comparisons, however incomplete, are likely to be of particular benefit for assessing the effectiveness of place promotion.

# 8 City marketing in practice

The concepts, processes and techniques described above have been operationalised by practitioners, within particular organisations established to achieve specific goals in necessarily individual urban situations. The nature of the organisation and its working methods is inevitably influenced by the adoption of marketing processes, while equally the sort of techniques adopted will be strongly influenced by the form of organisation operating them. This chapter will examine the relationship between organisation and process, illustrating in particular both the active and reactive roles fulfilled by the organisation.

## City marketing: a tradition refreshed

Linking generalisation with case example is rendered more than usually difficult by the inevitable uniqueness of each organisation considered. Nevertheless the adoption of city marketing and the subsequent evolution of a set of working methods and practices has been predominantly a matter of evolution from varied practical experience rather than the application of a standardised and widely accepted body of theory or technique. The preceding chapters may present a misleadingly consistent and systematic presentation from which it should not be concluded that particular local agencies have only to select appropriate applications from an existing menu. In terms of the historical development of this approach the reverse has more usually occurred, and most of the foregoing analysis has been derived as generalisation from practice. Therefore reference to a range of case studies has a particular importance.

The relationships between market planning and the planning organisations who implement and control them are complex and can be viewed from two standpoints. First, market planning as an approach has become almost inextricably entwined with the establishment of a number of deliberately created organisations, themselves sometimes linked to particular political ideologies, and representing ostensible marketing-derived solutions to urban planning problems. Here the idea of market planning is seen as an intrinsic concomitant of such organisations, to the extent that it becomes difficult to separate the two. Secondly, the reverse relationship may historically have occurred, namely that the adoption of the process has led to modifications in the structure, methods and ethos of the organisation, whether consciously intended or not and whether considered desirable in themselves or not. In both cases, but especially the former, the market planning organisation is itself an instrument of change by its demonstration of intent quite apart from its actual impacts through its measures upon the planning situation of the place concerned. Both of these relationships are important and will be pursued further.

Market planning has become popularly associated with specific types of organisations mostly established in the last few years. Whether the shift, detectable in a number of Western European countries in dominant planning philosophies, was a result of fundamental changes in dominant political ideologies, as part of a pervading 'anti-collectivism' or merely a disillusioned exasperation among practitioners and politicians alike that intractable urban problems had not appreciably been mitigated by previous planning approaches, was discussed earlier. The consequence, however, is that such a shift has led to a range of new agencies with new approaches. These often self-consciously draw upon the personnel, finance and organisational structures of the private sector, while publicly favouring ostensible market approaches. While both the adoption of market planning techniques and the establishment of particular agencies are both responses to the same trends, there is a distinct difference, and it is not sufficient just to present the new agencies as obvious cases of the application of best-practice marketing in public urban planning. Such an exclusive use of specially created market–oriented agencies would ignore the contribution of a much older market planning tradition and even more seriously contains the assumption that place marketing approaches are confined to such planning agencies: it is precisely in 'conventional' public authorities that the most important market planning, at least in terms of its spatial coverage, is to be found. In any event it is a central theme of this book that marketing has just such a role to play and should not be quarantined in specialised purposefully created agencies, whether public or private. It also cannot be assumed that the new specialist agencies are completely, or even in many cases dominantly, operating as market planning organisations in the way described earlier: in practice this is frequently not the case and new terminologies and even new partnership structures may conceal little more than traditional operating planning practices.

## From processes to organisations

There is no necessary and inevitable connection between any particular approach to public sector urban planning, on the one side, and the adoption of a particular organisational structure to implement it, on the other. The techniques described in Chapter 3 could logically be undertaken by organisations whose terms of reference, working methods, internal structures of authority and responsibility, guiding norms and values, measures of efficiency and systems of accountability were all pre-existing, having been developed for the application of quite different planning procedures. Indeed this is more often the case than the exception within public authorities, and easily explained by the relatively recent adoption of marketing approaches by most types of public authority where it would be unrealistic to expect long–established organisational structures, and, even more so, the personnel long accustomed to other techniques who staff them, to be instantly replaced with each such change.

Relevant questions in this respect are:

1.  Does the adoption of marketing approaches have, if not inevitable then at least likely, consequences, inherent in, and stemming from, the techniques themselves, at least in the longer term, for the organisations making use of them? If so, these consequences, intended or not, should be made explicit.
2.  Are particular organisational forms either necessary or helpful for the successful implementation of these approaches? If so, the nature of such structures should obviously be identified.

Answers to the first set of questions can be found in part in the processes described in Chapter 3 and in part in the history of the development of marketing as an applied science.

It was implicit in a number of stages of the iterative planning process (see Figure 3.4) that success is dependent upon an adaptation of aspects of the organisation to the requirements of the market through the process of auditing. Both the external, but more especially the internal, auditing techniques, described in Chapter 4, require an examination of the strengths and weaknesses of the service-producing agencies in the context of performance within the competitive market.

Although it is beyond our brief to examine the nature and operation of public sector organisations as such, an assessment of the organisational effects of such auditing requires the establishment of sets of contrasts relevant to our purposes that derive from alternative organisational models.

*Types of organisation*

Much of the discussion of the organisational implications of the adoption of marketing processes within public sector agencies assumes that organis-ations can be simply categorised within a public–private dichotomy. This distinction is laden with implied contrasts in the organisational objectives, strategies, working methods, systems of accountability and means of monitoring of success. A simple contrast is too often assumed to exist self-evidently, including from time to time in this book, and lies at the heart of many of the arguments both for and against the adoption of market planning. The reality is generally much less clear-cut than is frequently assumed which has implications for the description of suitable market planning structures.

The founding studies of public administration based their definitions upon the contrast between the judicial frameworks that defined the goals and structured the operation of public authorities: contrasting these with the absence of such legal constraints in private organisations operating in a free market (White, 1926). From this distinction grew the two separate lines of study which became public administration and business management respectively. The breaking down of the barriers between these had begun early in the inter-war period, especially in the United States, which rapidly led to a blurring of the boundaries between these disciplines as ideas, techniques and personnel were increasingly interchanged between them. The import of management ideas from the private sector is thus no novelty for public sector agencies, and recent interest in marketing science can be viewed as only the latest in a long tradition.

Even the much drawn contrast between bureaucratic and market accountability, with all the consequences for the organisation that are claimed to result from this, has been widely questioned. Galbraith (1967) popularised doubts about the traditional assumptions of the existence of a fundamental goal of profit-maximisation among private firms. The pursuit of survival, or maintenance of control, is substituted as being more typical of late capitalist oligarchy, than the models of Adam Smith derived from early competitive capitalism. Although not without notable dissent, personified by Friedman (1970) in particular, it is now conventional wisdom that the actual as opposed to stated goals, and thus working methods, of many private firms, especially the larger ones, may differ little from public sector organisations. Similarly the traditional definitions of bureaucracy and professionalism (see Weber, 1947) in which the former seeks validation and justification through an incumbent hierarchy, while the latter relates to the norms of an expert role-model group, would apply to the operation of many private as much as public organisations.

Thus the organisational consequences of the adoption of marketing approaches occur within a tradition of convergence and are thus neither so new, nor so radical in their implications, as might be expected. The organisational categories discussed below therefore relate to working practices rather than to legal status: many private organisations may operate bureaucratically, in a Weberian sense, while many public agencies may equally have a sustained history of entrepreneurialism within markets.

Within this spectrum the organisations discussed below can be broadly allocated to three categories, namely:

1. Public authorities with dominantly collective public interest goals for a part operating within selected free markets for particular services;
2. agencies, whether public or private, operating as competitive promotional organisations for certain activities, with limited responsibilities, detached from, but related to, public authorities with wider interests;
3. partnerships whether public-public or public-private, operating at various scales with various divisions of responsibility for finance, operation and control, for collective goals.

Despite the large quantity of recent descriptive work on the structure and operation of *public-private partnerships* (see, for example, Fostler and Berger (1982), Brooks *et al.* (1984), Davis (1986), Lemstra (1987), van Zandvoort (1989)) no one standard form of such a partnership has emerged as a general model, and almost every case described remains a more or less unique response to an equally unique set of planning problems and distinctive history of local experience in attempting to resolve them. Bussink (1988), for example, distinguishes eight different levels of co-operation. In order of increasing intensity, these are:

1. mutual awareness;
2. possibility of communication/common understanding;
3. discussions about activities;
4. consultation about activities and plans;
5. common participation in decision-making;
6. declaration of mutual intent;
7. collaboration contract;
8. establishment of joint company.

One of the two last mentioned forms of co-operation will be chosen when both the public and private parties carry a strong financial involvement with associated high risks.

The vast amount of literature on public-private partnership shows that a successful collaboration between governmental authorities and private firms is rarely a simple matter. In most cases a large number of conditions have to be met (see also Dijkstra, 1989). These fall into five main categories:

1. Relational conditions:
   (a) good social contacts between parties;
   (b) mutual trust;
   (c) sufficient flexibility of approach;

(d) enough certainty about the durability of the relationship;
(e) effective decision-making procedures.
2. Governmental-political conditions:
   (a) approval of political representatives;
   (b) provision of mandatory rights to political executives;
   (c) sufficient guarantees for the rights of third parties.
3. Legal conditions:
   (a) make explicit the rights and duties of all parties concerned;
4. Organisational conditions:
   (a) a proper shaping and phasing of the project;
   (b) effective regulation of managerial tasks.
5. Financial-economic conditions:
   (a) capital contribution of parties and investors;
   (b) a method of risk-sharing;
   (c) a method of profit-sharing;
   (d) financial constructions;
   (e) bookkeeping and inspection of financial accounts.

The implementation of these conditions is extremely important for a successful preparation of public-private projects. This implies that these aspects should be discussed at an early stage of the project development process.

Such a project development process is generally phased in five steps namely: initiative, preparation, financing, implementation and finally operation and management (see Table 8.1). As we have discussed in

**Table 8.1**   Stages in a project development process

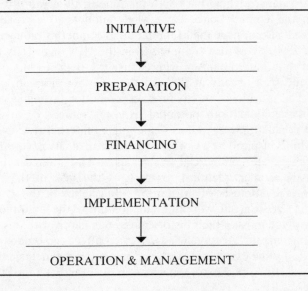

Chapter 3, the initiative phase may have a complex structure, being itself an iterative process as shown in Figure 3.4. Evidently, a market-oriented planning process at the urban level is usually directed towards realisation of the initiative phase of the project development process. However, the further the planning and development process advances, the more important becomes the regulating of activities and the less important becomes the incentive, or will-shaping, role of planning.

## Cases

It is not our brief to illustrate the structure and operation of all, or even a representative sample of, public authorities, whether existing or newly created, that make use of market planning, but to investigate the way such approaches and techniques as discussed in Chapters 3–7 are put into practice, and to draw conclusions from such practice about their effectiveness. The limited selection has been chosen in order to illustrate something of the variety of possibilities and the lessons suggested by either success or failure, in so far as these can be detected. In particular the importance ascribed to certain standard role-models in exerting a disproportionate influence on imitators is examined.

*Some early precursors*

Many of the characteristics of market planning as described above can be detected in the policies of public authorities well before the Second World War and even stretching back into the nineteenth century. For example, cities in the United States have what amounts to a tradition of 'city boosterism' almost since their foundation as competing pioneer settlements (Sadler, 1990). This idea stemmed from the view of the city as a 'growth machine', i.e. an organism whose survival depends upon continuous expansion, most usually at the expense of other cities in a competitive system. This is achieved by city product promotion through a wide range of media, targeted at both potential external sources of investment and resident populations, as well as sustaining an internal civic awareness and pride. This is inspired by a working partnership of city government officials and local private commercial businesses, whose interests in continuous growth are seen as identical; or at least the task of the former is to represent the interests of the latter. Many cities in the United States, ranging in size from a few thousand inhabitants to the largest in the country would through most of their history have been happy with this definition of city management: 'the organised effort to affect the outcome of growth distribution is the essence of local government as a dynamic political force' (Molotoch, 1976, p. 313). Organisations such as 'Atlanta Promotion' or

'Memphis Downtown Association', both funded and operated by local business interests and engaging in both external promotional boosterism and playing an active consultative role in local government decision-making, could be duplicated in many if not most US cities.

The nature of the urban tourism function has particularly encouraged the application of market management approaches, most evident in resort towns with a clear economic dependence upon this activity. The mix of public and private facilities that comprise the tourism package, together with the dominance of small firms, encouraged the assumption of a co-ordinating role by local authorities, generally in some form of partnership with private interests. Similarly the volatile nature of tourism demand, together with the intangibility of the product, equally encouraged the use of marketing as an instrument of management by such authorities, either in their own name or that of some local *ad hoc* 'Tourism Association'. Brown (1985; 1988), for example, has described the operation of local authorities as entrepreneurs both in the marketing of their own products and in their co-ordination of tourism services produced by others for cases dating from as early as the eighteenth century: '. . . almost since the beginning of the modern seaside resort in Britain deliberate promotion and marketing has been undertaken and . . . many resorts owe both their initial foundation and subsequent growth entirely to such activities' (1988, p. 176).

The methods are often crude by modern standards and their effectiveness constrained by the existing contemporary communications media, but the very existence of most of the elements necessary for market planning as described earlier at least dispels any notion that such approaches are an innovation of recent decades.

*The modern large scale role-models*

However, despite the existence of numerous, at least partial examples from a more distant past, it was the revitalisation efforts of a number of major cities in the United States during the 1970s that captured the imagination of a generation of urban planners, disillusioned by their own lack of spectacular success, and were imported messianically, if somewhat uncritically, as role-models especially into Western Europe in the course of the 1980s.

The essential attractive feature of these cases was the seeming dramatic economic restructuring of major conurbations whose traditional industries were in severe contraction, through the reshaping of the urban image held by both external private investors and by the urban communities themselves. Such restructuring occurred through what were presented as radical new approaches to the management of such cities, reflected in new market-oriented philosophies and operating structures designed to represent these. The adoption of these approaches was reinforced by federal government policies, especially the institution of the *Urban Development Action Grants*, available from national sources only on the condition that substantial matching sums of private investment were involved, and that an element of commercial return was ultimately to be expected from the programmes supported.

The central common elements in the revitalisation strategies, such as for Baltimore (e.g. de Jong and Lambooy, 1986; Falk, 1986; Allaert, 1989a), reflect the major features of market planning described earlier. These were innovatory management institutions, designed to allow the operation of the new coalition of local politicians and private investors, whether local or from outside the city; creative financing made possible by such quasi-public or mixed public/private agencies, replacing a dependence upon public subsidy by what was called the *leverage effect*, i.e. the obtaining of at least matching, and preferably far more than matching, investments from private sources, as a result of initial public contributions; leadership producing clearly defined and widely publicly accepted goals, emanating from both this coalition of the political and business communities; and an emphasis upon promotion both as a necessary precondition for shaping such a collective *civic consciousness* and then projecting it as a positive incentive for new development initiatives whether financed privately or publicly, from outside.

*Pittsburgh and Cleveland*    The cases of Pittsburgh and Cleveland are frequently taken as spectacular examples of a complete economic 'turn-round' achieved with the help of city marketing (see Holcomb, 1990), and deserve closer attention if only because local economies were restructured from smoke–stack to service base, and the principal activity of city governments was ostensibly market planning. In Pittsburgh the public-private partnership was reasserted as the central strategy at the 'Allegheny Conference' of self-styled local leaders (meaning in practice local business interests) in 1982. The three main results of this conference were the establishment of a marketing agency for encouraging inward commercial investment, the funding of a venture capital scheme to aid newly located enterprises, and the creating of a programme for attracting federal contracts and grants. This last is interesting both specifically in the US context where much federal aid is in fact the placement of national procurement contracts, and, as will be mentioned below in the European context, where some of the justification for the creation of public-private contracts is actually the improved chances of obtaining extra-urban public funding that result: leverage on the public purse may be as important as obtaining private investment. Cleveland's experience was very similar, with the 'Greater Cleveland Growth Association', composed basically from the chamber of commerce, playing the same roles. The various sets of

agencies conceived of their functions in much the same ways
the 'Greater Pittsburgh Office of Promotion', the 'Urban Re
Authority of Pittsburgh', the 'Penn's South-West Associat
'Neighborhood for Living Centers', were advertising and pul
agencies, concentrating on the shaping and propagation of
images. The role of the public authorities was limited and sup, ...ive but
rarely initiatory.

The difference between these campaigns of the 1980s and the earlier
'boosterism' endemic in US cities is mainly that they are better financed,
more professionally conducted, and above all more sophisticated in their
targeting at specific 'life-style defined groups' (e.g. Cleveland's campaigns
directed at 'young professionals' or 'business women').

*Assessment of the US models*   The criticisms of the operation of this
market-oriented urban planning in the US role-models have taken longer
to import and local misgivings have rarely been heard above the paeans of
praise for the obvious and highly visible successes. The goals of economic
development, and more especially the distribution of the costs and benefits
of such development among citizens can be, and almost from the beginning
of such projects have been, questioned (Harvey, 1989) and not only from
those with opposing views on the purposes of urban planning as a whole.
Of particular concern here are the areas of difficulty and weakness that
have been revealed in the practice of such planning. Many of these focus
specifically on the public-private management agencies which occupy such
a central role in all these strategies. These can be, and arguably by their
responsive nature must be, too numerous, vaguely defined in terms of
responsibilities, overlapping and even competing for funds. In Los Angeles
the efforts of the local authorities to generate economic development since
1980 have resulted in, 'a complex web of inner city programs, special
employment measures, enterprise initiatives, projects and regional
incentives . . .' (Miller, 1989). Similarly a theme that recurs in accounts of
different cities is that the existing institutions and mechanisms of public
planning are frequently in practice too weak in terms of manpower,
expertise, legal instrumentation and perhaps also self-confidence within
the local political climate of opinion in American cities to sustain a public–
private partnership, if the word 'partnership' is to retain any sense of
equality between the partners. Wolman (1986), writing about Detroit for
example, has pointed to the uncertainty of local public planners about
overall development goals, illustrated by the vascillation between job
creation and tax base expansion, as well as their lack of expertise in project
execution which reduces their role within partnership agencies to such
matters as land acquisition for private development and attempts to
mitigate the disruptive consequences of such development. The clear
successes of these US cities in radically restructuring their employment
bases, and also changing the physical appearance of many city centres

cannot be denied and the change in image, architecture and often vitality especially of parts of the central cities, of places such as Pittsburgh, Cleveland or Baltimore is nothing short of revolutionary (e.g. see Bailey, 1989). What is denied here, however, is that this has occurred solely, or even largely, as a result of city marketing in the sense explained in Chapter 3. Thus the wider relevance of these role-models to public authorities must be questioned.

## A Canadian middle way?

Although such revitalisation initiatives could not fail to be impressive in many cases in terms of both the scale and dramatic results that could be demonstrated, they do not represent as radical a departure from North American planning practice as was imagined by many Europeans. North American urban planning has traditionally been far more dependent upon the practice of negotiation of development rights between public and private interests, and the resolution of potential conflicts through trade-offs than has been the case in most of Western Europe, if only as a result of the essential weakness of enforceable legislative instruments and the existence of local authority planning within a free market ethos.

The relationship between collectively established objectives and market-oriented management techniques is well illustrated by some Canadian *Crown Corporations*. These operate within the Canadian political context in which a larger measure of public intervention for collective goals is generally more acceptable than in the United States, although the same broad context of a free market is assumed to exist (Hodge, 1985). The Toronto Harbourfront Corporation, for example, first established as a public agency in 1972 and incorporated as a Crown Corporation in 1978 (Desfors *et al.*, 1988), in response to the existence of large quantities of potential development land in a critical area of the inner city, alongside the lake shore, as a result of the progressive abandonment of railway and dockside uses (see Figure 8.1). The public planning involvement is reflected both in its establishment by the federal government and its reliance on the local authority for development consent. Collective goals are reflected clearly in its mandate which is to 'develop the harbourfront site in accordance with a development framework approved by the crown (i.e. the public interest) and to initiate cultural and recreational programmes of public benefit.' The methods by which this is to be achieved, however, are basically those of the market in so far as the corporation is dominantly self-financing, using profits from commercial and residential developments to cross-subsidise non-profit making enterprises in the public interest. The balance struck between the reliance on the private investment market and the attainment of public goals is constantly changing (see Table 8.2) as 'the details of the market driven redevelopment, such as its pace, extent and

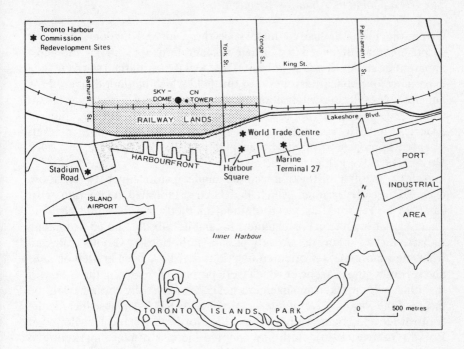

**Figure 8.1** . *Toronto Harbourfront*

composition are mediated by the local political system and the corporate interests of local proprietary institutions' (Ashworth and Sijtsma, 1990, p. 33).

**Table 8.2** Balance of public and private revenues and expenditures for Toronto Harbourfront Corporation 1980–97 (Toronto Harbourfront Corporation, 1988)

| Income 1980–97 | | 1980–8 | 1988–9 | 1990–7 |
|---|---|---|---|---|
| Public activities | 26 | 30 | 46 | 37 |
| Development | 30 | 67 | 51 | 44 |
| Government grants | 45 | 3 | 4 | 19 |
| | | | | |
| EXPENSES | | | | |
| Public activities | 44 | 67 | 74 | 62 |
| Development | 10 | 10 | 11 | 11 |
| Capital improvements | 46 | 23 | 15 | 27 |

*The UK alphabet of urban regeneration*

Given the urban industrial history of the United Kingdom, it is not surprising that the need for urban regeneration was among the most apparent of all developed countries. This, together with the relatively long experience of public intervention in this field which had not delivered the anticipated results in revitalisation and the election in 1979 of a government committed to radical approaches, explains the early proliferation of agencies, initiatives and programmes which promised a more market-oriented approach to public urban planning (Young and Mason, 1983; Hoyle *et al.*, 1988) (Figure 8.2).

Among these a distinction can be made historically between those agencies already existing, which had been established to operate what came to be regarded as the traditional methods of urban and regional planning, such as acting as channels for public subsidy and co-ordinating the activities of other, dominantly public, authorities at various scales, to which new more market-oriented functions may have been grafted on later and secondly, those agencies which were purposely created in the course of the 1980s with market management goals. Amongst the former could be included the *Regional Development Authorities* (RDAs). These include the Scottish Development Authority and the Northern Ireland Development Board (Gulliver, 1989). Both had adopted the task of place marketing to attract inward private investment as a state function in 1975 and aimed at a ratio of around 60:40 public:private balance of investment. The SDA's most notable excursion in urban development, its involvement and sponsoring of the Glasgow GEAR project, had distinct echoes of the North American models in its stress upon image promotion (in practice negative image correction), not only for the attraction of inward investment but as a means of shaping a distinctive civic identity and raising self-confidence (Hart and Harrison, 1990).

Similarly amongst the newly created market-oriented programmes there were examples of some of what have been termed non-planning or even anti-planning responses, such as the twenty-five *Enterprise Zones* (EZs) established after 1980 (Lawless, 1986), and *Simplified Planning Zones* (SPZs) since 1987, whose commitment to market approaches was theoretically so complete as to consist principally of the removal of planning controls and thus these cannot be classified as market planning approaches at all.

The clearest cases of new organisations specifically established for the implementation of a new market–led approach to urban planning were the *Urban Development Corporations* (UDCs) introduced in 1980. These were to be 'the forefront of the government's drive to revitalise the inner city . . . through a single minded private sector oriented approach to urban regeneration' (DOE, 1987). Of the first two established in 1981, in the East London Docklands and on Merseyside, the former, the London Docklands

**Figure 8.2**   *UK Urban Programmes*
*Urban Development Corporations ('stars')*
*Enterprise Zones ('triangles')*
*Urban Programme Authorities ('squares')*

Development Corporation (LDDC) was from its inception regarded by opponents and proponents alike as the tangible flagship of the new government–sponsored approach to the problems of inner city revitalisation, and as such has received a great deal of attention either critical or adulatory ever since. This close attention is a result in part of the sheer physical extent of its area of responsibility, in part the enormity of the problem of economic decline and environmental dereliction that it attempted to tackle, and not least a result of 'the most aggressive, expensive and sophisticated public relations, marketing and advertising programmes ever mounted on behalf of a local authority in Britain' (Burgess and Wood, 1988, p. 97), or it could be added almost anywhere else in Europe. It is not surprising therefore that the LDDC became a more impressive and relevant role-model of market-oriented planning organisations for Western Europe, than the older United States examples.

The LDDC, however, was only one of the ten corporations established and in a number of respects it was quite untypical. The most obvious of these is size and the resulting importance to central government credibility and high media profile, both of which conferred automatic advantages in access to both public and private investments. In addition all the other UDCs were located in conurbations typified by declining nineteenth–century heavy industries with few of the compensating growth sectors in tertiary and quaternary services, such as those which had proved so important in generating commercial and residential demands in the Docklands. The leverage ratio of 1:10, public to private investment in the LDDC, was only approached in Manchester's Trafford park (1:7) with the figures for Cardiff Bay (1:4), and Tyne and Wear (1:2) being much lower, and Merseyside being so low (7:1) as to question the use of the term (Stoker, 1989).

However, they all share the elements of a market–oriented strategy, including boards representing a partnership of public and private interests with wide responsibilities and powers including both the traditional local authority functions of development control, land management and subsidy distribution as well as the new initiatory and entrepreneurial roles, with a high priority being given to shaping and then promoting what is seen as a climate encouraging of both local and externally attracted enterprise. One of the three goals is 'to encourage the development of industry and commerce', and specifically for the public sector to initiate but to 'encourage subsequent development of land by the private sector' (DOE, 1987). The Tyne and Wear UDC summarised its function as, 'we are not a plan-led organisation, our role is to guide and focus market forces' (quoted in Sadler, 1990).

Although the UDCs represent the clearest case of the direct and deliberate application of market planning approaches within urban regions, there are many other developments at various scales with similar characteristics. Such as the more specific *City Grants* (CGs) intended 'to support private sector capital projects in run-down urban areas' (DOE, 1987), and the *Urban Programme*, again specifically designed to make assistance available for private sector projects which contribute towards urban economic development, 'thereby enabling investors to make a reasonable return' (DOE, 1987). There are in addition a number of Urban Development ment Agencies (UDAs) not specifically linked to any of the above national programmes, although they may obtain funding from many public and private sources, which are direct partnerships between one local authority and a number of private firms and even individuals. The 'Birmingham Heartlands', for example (Beeston, 1989), operates as a limited company, within which the local authority holds 35 per cent of the share capital.

The role of national governments in encouraging the establishment of new development agencies at the urban level and stimulating the adoption of market-oriented approaches through such enabling programmes is well represented by the UK cases described briefly above, if anything even more so than in the American examples. There is in addition, however, a further scale that has been a significant stimulus in part of Western Europe, namely the supra-national scale of the European Community structural funds. The *European Regional Development Fund* (ERDF) and to a much lesser extent the *European Social Fund* (ESF) and *European Investment Bank* (EIB) have distributed steadily growing sums to European conurbations (21 thousand million ECUs annually by 1989) principally in support of economic restructuring and environmental renewal programmes. Tapping these funds has become an understandable preoccupation of local urban authorities and success in obtaining such support has become increasingly a determining condition for success for large–scale urban revitalisation. Such success is more likely to be obtained if the fragmented public agencies and authorities within conurbations can present a common coherent and integrated programme, capable of being executed through an established common agency, and can demonstrate the strength of existing national public support and access to local private investments (Penny, 1989). These responses have been formalised in the UK in the *Integrated Development Operations* (IDOs), 11 of which are in various stages of preparation in 1990 and three have been formally approved. The majority of these are found in the industrial conurbations of Northern England, Strathclyde and industrial South Wales.

One of the earliest established, and so far most successful, of these IDOs is the Manchester, Salford, Trafford IDO, in North-West England, phased to operate between 1989–93. This is basically a public sector led programme, or more properly a set of five interlocking programmes, called 'strategic objectives', each of which is both a public-private and equally important public-public, partnership between different agencies. Despite the importance of the public local authorities in the initiative and execution of the objectives, generally called 'strategic initiatives', three persistent themes, each of which can be regarded as a hallmark of market approaches

**Table 8.3** Action programmes of the MST IDO (after Green, 1989)

| Action programme | Title (content) |
| --- | --- |
| A | Rejuvenation of older industrial areas (mostly infrastructural improvement and site preparation) |
| B | Tourism and Culture (dominantly heritage and cultural activities) |
| C | Business development and support (enterprise support, development initiatives, managed workshops, etc.) |
| D | Communications (mainly road improvements of regional importance) |
| E | Environment (amenity improvement, landscaping, etc.) |
| F | Workforce and training (retraining and reskilling) |

are apparent in the reports of the IDO (Green, 1989). These are partnerships at both national and local levels (under the slogan 'effective partnership works'); the successful competition with other locations for private inward investment, mainly through action to reverse existing negative images of the region and the city; and thirdly, the recognition of the importance of small and medium-sized enterprises, most of which already exist within the region and have strong contacts with it, which are to be provided with 'enterprise support' which in practice is largely marketing assistance. There is in addition a re-emphasis on some of the conventional tasks of land-use planning (see the 'action programmes' in Table 8.3), but with a significantly different justification, namely the shaping of an environment attractive to inward investment and the physical rejuvenation of derelict and unsightly areas which contribute towards the existing detrimental image of the area.

It is somewhat ironic that the need to obtain EC subsidies, in competition with other needy areas, has been so influential in shaping effective partnerships, devising integrated programmes and adopting many of the techniques and personnel of private rather than public sector organisations, while the subsidy granting international organisation is itself notable for its complex bureaucratic procedures and lack of integration, which the restructuring of the funds in 1989 went only some way towards correcting.

Similarly, the Organisation for Economic Cooperation and Development (OECD), in particular, promotes what it calls 'positive adjustment policies', i.e. economic restructuring, and quite explicitly encourages 'broader more effective and more innovative capital markets' (Penny, 1989, p. 1), including specifically the 'stimulation of venture capital'. The Organisation has an advice rather than subsidy granting role and therefore is much less influential than the EC funds in shaping new local agencies geared to funding possibilities, but is important in propagating what might be termed current acceptable practice, which in recent years given its membership has been strongly market oriented.

This brief description of the presence of marketing approaches found within the recent and purposely established urban agencies within one country is an incomplete account of the importance of market planning among urban public authorities if only because existing local authorities may merely add new responsibilities, procedures or approaches to those already in existence. Such new approaches may be reflected in the establishment of specialised departments within the authority often on an *ad hoc* basis, although staffed internally and generally within internal hierarchical structures, and financial systems. There are distinct promotional advantages in the adoption of identifiable names (with the accompanying logos and slogans). Stockport's Economic Enterprise Area, for example, is neither an official EZ nor recipient of any of the nationally funded programmes described above, but a development department of the local authority, staffed largely from the existing planning department, with a brief to attract and assist private sector investment.

Equally there may be no particular new organisational structures reflecting an authority's exploration and experimentation with market planning. At the city level the conclusions of the Glasgow authority on its current position and future prospects in the competition for inward commercial investment (City of Glasgow, 1989) is undoubtedly not untypical of many such reports circulating within local authorities, which in turn have led to the adoption of market-oriented policies, mainly for attracting inward investment, in a number of existing civic policies executed by existing departments within existing organisational structures. An account of the application of the framework presented in Chapter 3 as an additional element in more traditional structure planning techniques, at the county scale, is described by Clarke (1985) for Gwent.

*Some other national experiences*

Although the UK provides a remarkable range of newly created agencies ostensibly implementing a variety of aspects of market planning, experience elsewhere in Europe offers some illuminating contrasts.

*The Netherlands*    The international reputation of the Netherlands for a strong commitment to centrally led physical and economic planning, executed through a hierarchy of planning authorities (e.g. see Voogd, 1982; Alexander, 1988), makes the Dutch experience of particular interest. The national government commitment to the introduction of a stronger marketing element into planning was articulated in the publication of the Fourth National Report on Physical Planning by the National Planning Agency (*Rijksplanologische Dienst*) in 1988. In sharp contrast to the three previous national reports published since 1960, which had been principally concerned with rectifying regional inequalities and constraining and directing the spatial consequences of growth, the new policy emphasised the need for planning to help shape the conditions within which further growth could be encouraged to occur. The Dutch cities were seen to exist within two markets, engaged in competition both nationally with each other, and internationally (or specifically within a post-1992 European arena) with other urban agglomerations for the location of higher order quaternary services (e.g. see Janssen and Machielse, 1988, for a Dutch, or DATAR, 1989, for a continent-wide view of this competitive arena). Regional policy which previously had consisted very largely of the transfer of subsidies from the areas of growth to the economically lagging regions, now consisted in essence of little more than exhortations from the centre that the periphery must seek economic growth through the exploitation of its own local regional markets. To this end the largest cities, or agglomerations of cities, were designated as urban nodes, which were to be foci of regional economic enterprise. The influence of the RPD on the lower provincial and district authorities is considerable, not so much through the production of a national physical blueprint to which the plans of subordinate authorities must conform, as through the conditioning of a climate of ideas and professional conventional wisdom.

A survey of Bartels and Timmer (1987) set out to describe the extent to which city marketing, however defined, was being practised within local authorities in the Netherlands and sampled 198 district authorities (*gemeenten*). Although these were a minority of the national total of 714 at that time, they did include all the urban authorities. One hundred and sixty admitted using city marketing techniques. Further investigation revealed that marketing was in practice interpreted in almost all cases to mean promotion, and such promotion was dominantly directed outside the authority concerned and targeted, albeit often vaguely, mainly at inward investment (see also Buursink and Borchert, 1987). Municipal budgets allocated to these activities had increased an average sevenfold between 1980 and 1987, and were spent principally on media advertising (32 per cent), producing and distributing promotional materials (21 per cent) and exhibitions (17 per cent).

A conclusion of this study was that the size of the local authority determined not only whether marketing was attempted but equally the sort of marketing undertaken. The larger cities of the Western Netherlands in particular not only spent proportionally more but had a more complete grasp of the possibilities. Rotterdam, for example, had an extensive central area revitalisation plan based upon a theme of 'Water City' involving not only a reuse of vacant waterfront sites for cultural and recreational amenities, but the refurbishing of the city's industrial image through slogans such as 'Manhatten on the Maas'.

It is notable in the Dutch case, in contrast to that of the UK, that the emphasis on market approaches is to be found mainly within the existing public local authority structures, albeit assisted sometimes by private consultancies, rather than in specialised agencies set up with the encouragement of the national government, alongside, and often even in opposition to, the existing local democratically responsible municipalities and provinces. The case of the *Tourism Recreation Development Plans* (TROPs) reveals perhaps a distinctive Dutch contribution to the introduction of marketing approaches by conventional planning authorities through what appear to have much in common with conventional structure plans. The content of these plans, as described in Chapter 3, are notable by their reordering of the phasing of the planning process so as to begin with audits of the existing and potential markets of the place within an assumed competitive situation. There is no doubt, however, that these are publicly led plans that have been devised, and are to be executed, by public planning bodies at the provincial and district levels. The private sector has been consulted and is expected to finance many if not most of the tourism/recreation projects expected, and a large element of leverage is expected, probably over-optimistically (see Ashworth and Bergsma, 1987).

*Belgium*    A similar economic history has led to many Belgian cities having similar revitalisation problems to those of the UK (Allaert, 1989b). The structure of government and of public planning is, however, quite different and lacks much of the tradition of public intervention found in the Netherlands. Nevertheless an Act of 1988 specifically encouraged the establishment of public-private partnerships as a vehicle for urban regeneration, drawing explicitly on the experience of the United States, Canada and the United Kingdom. A whole range of urgent tasks was seen as being appropriate for such new agencies which would improve the competitive situation of the Belgian cities as a whole. These tasks, some of which were new but many of which had long been the responsibility of the existing local authorities, were the renewal of urban infrastructure, the establishment of new transport facilities to exploit European integration, especially the modernisation of ports and airports, the more cost-effective management of urban housing, especially in the inner urban areas built in the nineteenth century, as well as the promotion of 'culture' to markets within and outside the cities.

Although experience has been short, and only two large–scale comprehensive projects are in progress, namely at Gent (North Flank Development) and the Ostend waterfront, some fundamental misgivings have emerged. First, and most fundamental, the division of responsibility within the partnerships was intended to give the initiative to the public authorities and the financing (at least for around 80 per cent of costs) to the private sector. In practice neither has proved capable of the task allocated which casts doubt upon the whole nature of the partnership. The existing structure of local government has proved to be too weak, in manpower, instrumentation and even wider credibility to initiate large–scale revitalis-ation projects and obtain sufficient financial support from private sources. Secondly, the existence of a strong element of political ideology behind the drive to adopt market-oriented planning, and its encouragement by the national government, has introduced a degree of vulnerability (see also De Decker, 1989). Change in the composition of that government, which in a country with a tradition of shifting coalition administrations means that both the ideology and the encouragement are unlikely to outlast the time it takes to initiate and execute urban projects.

Although the cases considered above are too recent for experience to be distilled into a series of clear-cut lessons, nevertheless some tentative general conditions for success have emerged and these can be outlined in the next chapter.

# 9 City marketing: an interim assessment

A paradox that has emerged more than once in the preceding chapters is that, on the one side, there is nothing specifically novel about applying marketing to publicly managed services and even to the promotion of places as a whole: the basic ideas are not only logically simple but often effectively self-evident and it would have been remarkable if public agencies had consistently failed to appreciate that they have markets for their services and that they inevitably exist within some form of competitive arena. On the other hand, the self-conscious adoption of techniques and philosophies from marketing science as place management instruments for the achievement of collectively determined goals is new, and thereby suffers many of the consequences of this novelty. By its nature many of the applications discussed above are experimental and have become laden with the optimistic expectations associated with the pioneers and prophets of any new idea. Assessment requires mature and objective judgemental generalisations of the strengths, weaknesses, problems and further opportunities drawn from a wide range of results. Most of these conditions are unlikely to be met in such an experimental stage, however important to the further success of the experiments such assessment may be.

If a fundamental change in public authority management is occurring, then, as has been argued earlier, it is dominantly a 'bottom-up' revolution. Numerous, generally highly individualistic, applications of aspects of the marketing processes described are in progress, and few practitioners have the ability, time, or inclination to generalise from these fragmented experiences. Among the consequences of novelty, and inevitable concomitants of the early phases of the adoption of what appear to be revolutionary ideas, are both an optimistic overestimation of the likely benefits by the proponents and exaggerated, and often largely unfounded, misgivings of opponents. Both have a clear vested interest. The advocates of novelty must overstate their case to obtain acceptance of the possibility of experiment which cannot but provoke an overstatement of dangers among those committed to the maintenance of current practices. Both these reactions have been particularly apparent in the case of market planning approaches which has generated more than its fair share of misunderstandings, some of which have become so firmly entrenched as to deserve the title of myths.

Some of the more important of these are considered below as assessment must depend on more than over-optimistic hopes or unduly pessimistic fears. Once the negative barriers to assessment are removed, or at least can be understood sufficiently to be taken into account, the more positive question of what are then the preconditions for success can be considered.

## Some myths and misunderstandings

*City marketing is just old practices dressed in new terminologies*

The most obvious source of misunderstanding, that has been apparent in many guises throughout this book, is that the term city marketing is used to denote different levels of the application of marketing to public sector planning.

At its shallowest market planning can be just the importation of a new terminology derived from the commercial marketing of physical goods, which is substituted for more conventional terms. This may be regarded as a harmless manifestation of fashion in a professional argot, to which public planning has been particularly prone over the years. The danger is that the appearance of novelty may conceal the absence of substantive change and the opportunities offered by the approach will be lost.

On other occasions the marketing terms are accompanied by the adoption of procedures and techniques, sets of planning instruments which can be selected in appropriate circumstances, as an alternative to, or alongside, existing ones. At the extreme, city marketing can be reduced to a synonym of its most well-known instrument: thus city promotion, or narrower still, city advertising is practised divorced from the market and product management discussed in Chapters 4 and 5 respectively. In many of the organisations outlined in Chapter 8, especially those in existence before the late 1970s, city marketing is treated in this way, as a technique of spatial planning or even as a management procedure ordering the way city management policies are derived and applied.

More rarely are new concepts imported with the terminology and the techniques so that a distinctly different relationship between public services and their users is intended, with the resulting implications for the identification of urban problems, the devising of policies to tackle them and the way the results of such policies are assessed.

The difficulty is quite simply to know what meanings are attached to the term *marketing* when it is used in particular urban planning contexts and the possibility for misunderstanding is particularly evident.

*City marketing is an alternative to conventional development control
and structure planning*

There is frequently an implication that market planning supersedes other techniques, their terminology, skills and practices in urban planning, and especially that it is an alternative to a discredited regulatory land-use planning as a means of resolving functional conflict and allocating space within cities. This is undeniably partially the case in so far as marketing philosophies do imply a different set of working methods, forms of accountability and criteria of success. Equally there is substance to the argument that if a large measure of choice is performed by customers operating through markets then some of the justification for macro-scale structure planning is severely weakened.

However, reference back to the procedures of market planning, as defined here, reveals that there are a number of phases of product or customer management where the more traditional skills of regulatory land-use and physical structure planning not only remain but are actually required. For example land-use planning and landscaping and design are in themselves possible marketing strategies (as in Figure 3.1). Environmental amenity in various forms loomed large in many of the programmes of market-oriented agencies discussed in Chapter 8, with in every case the assumption being made that this was inevitably a public function exercised by public agencies in the public interest on the basis of collectively determined norms. The relationship between 'old' and 'new' is not so much the extinction of the former by the latter as old crafts become redundant, so much as a reordering within the planning process, or even the substitution of justifications derived from the new to provide renewed purposes for the skills of the old.

*City marketing is principally a means of attracting inward investment*

One of the earliest practised forms of city marketing was the attraction of exogenous investment. Foot-loose industries were to be encouraged to locate within an authority's boundaries rather than elsewhere. Such 'smoke-stack' hunting rapidly shifted targets to service industries whether public or private, as it became clear that 'smoke-stacks' were neither very plentiful nor perhaps even completely desirable, and the higher order quaternary services, offered both more desirable benefits, fewer unwanted local externalities, and were in any event more dependent in their locational decisions on precisely those amenity factors over which the authority had either direct control or believed it could influence most effectively. In addition such tasks could be relatively easily grafted on to the existing responsibilities of departments, or contracted out to independent agencies, without seriously disrupting the existing working methods or structures of the authority. Small wonder, therefore, that marketing was eagerly embraced by local authorities for this purpose, and became automatically associated with selling the city to new markets outside it. Although such an orientation has remained of importance, especially in such cases as new town corporations or new urban development agencies needing to establish their identity in external markets, it is obvious that existing markets will be proportionately of much more significance. In any event, although the pioneer authorities to engage in external marketing of their services may enjoy an advantage, once all municipalities are involved the result is a zero-sum gain, except on the rare occasions when an extension of the total demand can be envisaged as a result of total marketing activities. Defensive strategies designed to hold on to existing residents, firms and visitors are likely to be more important in the long run than any marginal additions to those attracted from other areas as a result of aggressive external strategies. For most urban authorities, most of the time, external markets are likely to be in reality of minimal importance compared with what can be termed *self-marketing*. Of the various strategic options discussed in Chapter 3, the most important is the use of marketing in the effective management of existing public services for existing citizens, whether currently users or not. Even in the more spectacular role–models discussed in Chapter 8, the shaping of a particular internal civic consciousness, renewed self-confidence, or local creativity and enterprise was generally more important than attracting new activities, investments or purchasers from outside.

*City marketing is selling what we have got*

When stated as baldly as this such a misunderstanding of the basic orientation of all marketing approaches is obvious. Clearly we have argued that market planning involves a definite switch in emphasis from a concentration on the management of the facility as such to one based upon the actual or potential user. Public services are satisfiers of needs for housing, transport or recreation rather than managers of housing stocks, bus fleets or swimming pools. However, the actual adoption of market planning has frequently occurred as a solution, and too often a last resort solution at that, to the problems of existing supply rather than as a response to anticipated demand. City marketing is often introduced into authorities with variations on the question, 'what can we do with our city?' (or worse 'how can we continue to finance our existing leisure centres, bus fleets or libraries by finding new users or uses?'). In marketing terms the question ought to be on the lines of , 'what markets can be found or created to buy the urban products that we are capable of producing or can become capable of producing, better than competitors?'. In other words marketing should attempt to adjust supply to demand rather than the reverse. The nature of public authorities, their accumulated responsibilities, properties and staffs, renders this difficult, especially when they are accountable within a local political system.

A clear example of the almost unavoidable nature of this mal-orientation is described for the field of urban conservation planning in Ashworth (1988). A stock of conserved buildings and artefacts has been accumulated in most Western European countries over the past 50 years by state agencies for a mix of motives, none of which were directly concerned with contemporary use; financial constraints in recent years have encouraged the *commodification* of publicly owned historic resources on various 'heritage' markets, sought out as a means of finding a commercial return for an existing largely immobile, and by its nature also largely immutable, supply. The attempt has been made to resolve similar dilemmas with similar solutions for existing municipal stocks of facilities as diverse as civic halls, libraries, sports centres, and even cemeteries.

Public sector organisations, unlike commercial firms, have often little choice but to begin with an existing resource and then seek a market for it, however heretical that might be in the terms of marketing science theory as presented in Chapters 1 and 2. But, as argued in Chapter 5, this requires at the very least the careful definition of the product or products, to be shaped from such resources in the context of market demands and not as frequently occurs the assumption that these are self-evident. Thus, as in the above example, the public caretakers of a conserved building are selling not castles or cathedrals but a particular packaged recreational or educational experience formed from these in reaction to the requirements of the market.

*City marketing is the introduction of commercialisation and privatisation into public services*

The link between marketing as a procedure and political ideologies favouring the free operation of markets is understandable if only because, as has been stressed, marketing science was historically developed within private firms for the selling of goods and services for profit. Its application within public planning introduced techniques, ways of regarding services and frequently also personnel from the private sector. These innovations could easily be seen as a move towards the *commercialisation* of public services, i.e. the use of direct market accountability as the measure of success and determinant of what and how services were to be operated in place of previously used professional or public service norms. Similarly it could be seen as being only a short logical step towards *privatisation*, i.e. the detachment of suitable services, previously operated by public agencies, to independent and self-financing organisations.

These assumptions about the implications of using marketing in public services have been compounded by the deliberate association of marketing with a strong element of political ideology. This association can be explained in part by coincidences of time and space. The early influential role models provided by the US cities described in Chapter 8 all stressed the operation of a public urban planning that had always been deeply embedded in a free enterprise culture, and which rarely questioned the assumptions of that culture, although it reduced planning to playing a supportive rather than initiatory role.

Similarly the introduction of marketing approaches in many Western European countries coincided with the election of governments committed to the expansion of free market ideologies at the expense of the public sector, as well as the imposition of constraints upon public expenditure, which in turn led to political pressures in a number of Western European countries in the course of the 1980s for the privatisation of many public services. Both the political right and left therefore used marketing terminology as slogans, and market-oriented planning agencies as symbols to be supported or opposed on ideological principle and developed vested interests in their success or failure.

Against such entrenched political interest we can only reiterate that what we have described in Chapters 3–7 is only a form of urban management that recognises that all services inevitably exist within markets, and uses that recognition to analyse the relationship of product and customer in order to maximise the efficiency of production and the satisfaction of the consumer. This in no way implies that the only acceptable market mechanism is that of cash price and the only measure of efficiency is immediate financial profit on the transaction. In the public services discussed above the predetermined goals remain for the most part collective goals, collectively determined, and their achievement is not necessarily or even usually, measurable in terms of direct monetary profits. The relationship of product and customer within markets does not have to be regulated through a monetary price paid by an individual customer in an individual transaction. Pricing exists, otherwise how can consumer choice be exercised within a competitive situation, but that pricing can be indirect and calculated in non-monetary units. City marketing could be described as 'marketing without markets' in the sense that it does require a different series of market mechanisms relating producer and consumer. Merely because these specific market mechanisms are different from those familiar in the commercial sector, and in addition often difficult to recognise, or to calibrate, does not in itself deny the existence of a market arrangement, only that it is different in kind.

Thus, although the process of the adoption of marketing ideas in public authorities has been accelerated in a number of countries by the existence of strong central government pressure powered by free market political ideologies, such a hijacking of city marketing is neither logically inevitable nor may be particularly desirable for the future of city marketing as a planning procedure. The strong association of any planning methodology with a particular political ideology carries with it a number of obvious intrinsic dangers. In plural democracies government support will be countered by opposition, leaving experiments in market planning vulnerable to changes of government, as has occurred in Belgium (Allaert, 1989b). Less dramatically the success of the application of marketing procedures is unlikely to be monitored dispassionately in the context of the planning problems to be solved, but will be judged against predetermined political stances. The danger is that much of the efficacy of the approach will thus be disregarded and the opportunity for the amelioration of long-term urban planning problems may be lost.

*City marketing is a solution to all urban problems*

Finally in this catalogue of widely–held misunderstandings is the idea that city marketing is a panacea which can be evoked as a solution in itself to a wide range of long-standing and so far intractable urban problems. When so simply stated such an assertion appears so patently ludicrous as to be hardly worth refuting. However, there is a sufficient element of such thinking detectable in some authorities to make a warning appropriate. There is a reductionism implicit in much of the rhetorical hyperbole of the agencies discussed in Chapter 8, that regards all urban problems as ultimately dependent for their solution upon economic revitalisation, which in turn is seen to be largely a question of retaining or attracting back, commercial firms. When reliance is being placed upon marketing as the principal means of achieving this, then the assumption that city marketing is being overloaded with unrealistic expectations is understandable.

It also needs stressing, especially in those governmental agencies where the adoption of marketing terminologies is little more than a thin cover for budgetary deficiencies, that city marketing as a procedure outlined in Chapter 3, is very largely a resource management technique, not a substitute for the existence of resources, whether of personnel, finance or creative ideas.

## The preconditions for success

Many of the preconditions for the likely success of market planning in public authorities are implicit in the description of procedures in Chapter 3 and the analysis of the components involved in Chapters 4–7: they equally emerged more explicitly from the case studies of organisation, structures, goals and achievements sketched in Chapter 8. It remains only to stress four final points that even at this relatively early stage in the application of this approach to public sector urban management can be identified, if not as absolute requirements for success, at least as conditions that make such success more probable.

*All or nothing*

City marketing has been subject to a number of different interpretations and has been presented in the above chapters in a variety of ways, reflecting a similar variety in its application. At times it is little more than an exercise in the renaming of public service providers, operations and users, which, while perhaps encouraging some redefinitions that may be refreshing and stimulating of new ideas, makes few fundamental demands upon public administration or administrators. At a deeper level, Chapter 3 can be taken as a whole to be a coherent management procedure which can be applied as if it were an operating manual by following the critical paths outlined in the various diagrams: or alternatively the chapter, together with those analysing products, markets, and images that follow could be used as a sort of tool-box, to be rummaged through in search of appropriate techniques as particular practical planning problems arise.

An interpretation that is at least ostensibly quite different is to be found among many of the agencies established with a deliberate commission to introduce aspects of the market into public sector planning. These have concentrated initially on the shaping of new administrative structures, from which new working methods that include an awareness of, and operations in, markets, are expected to develop: new partnerships of various sorts are defined and manifested through new divisions of responsibility, account-ability and executive authority.

The central question that arises is, can these various levels of possible application be treated as an à la carte menu from which a free selection can be made according to the nature of the planning problem to be tackled, or the predisposition of the planning authority? Alternatively, is a progress through the various levels inevitable as terminologies, concepts, procedures and philosophies are so bound together as to be imported with each other, whether willingly and consciously, or not? Expressed differently, is success in market planning dependent upon the application of the total package by agencies and individuals committed to the basic philosophy as a whole, or can relevant aspects be applied, disembodied from the rest, within quite different contexts?

The answer has appeared in different guises throughout many of the chapters. The procedures of Chapter 3 form a logical sequence that cannot be followed for only a part of its course: similarly the market investigation of Chapter 4, the product analysis of Chapter 5 and the promotional strategies of Chapter 7 are clearly interdependent: they cannot with success be applied separately.

*Limits to market planning*

The above plea that the various aspects of market planning are applied as a complete package rather than as disembodied parts does not deny, however, that it will be more appropriate to some aspects of urban management than others. Implicit in many of the arguments in the preceding chapters is the idea that it will be particularly apposite in those areas of public sector urban management where clear and quantifiable goals can be established, the service product is definable and the targeted consumer group is identifiable and accessible. Although there are many public services which fulfil such criteria satisfactorily, including many that are less usually considered to be suitable for marketing, there are equally many that do not, cannot and, probably for many reasons, should not, meet such requirements. The concept of the public interest as being more than the resultant of the aggregation of private interests may in some instances be either indefinable or inexpressible in terms of the market. Many so-called NIMBY ('not in my back yard') issues, for instance, would be difficult to resolve through market planning (Popper, 1981). There is thus a need for selectivity within public planning agencies and the skill at undertaking this is itself a major precondition for success.

*Structures and organisations*

The relationships between the adoption of an approach to planning and the structures and organisations established to operate it have been stressed throughout. Therefore it is clear that success will depend as much upon such arrangements for execution as the ostensible adoption of all the various procedures suggested in Chapters 3–7. That is not to argue that Chapter 8 should be regarded as a pattern book of possible partnership structures suitable for the operation of the techniques described and from which selection can be made. On the contrary, one conclusion of even such an incomplete survey of existing market-oriented planning agencies is that no model exists suitable for all occasions. Similarly many, if not all, successful applications of market-oriented procedures have occurred within traditional administrative structures. What seems to be important is what has been described as *the marketing gap*, i.e. the marketing within the organisation itself such as each department or individual is cognisant of the existence of the appropriate markets, the nature of the products being supplied and the goals of the organisation and each of the departments producing them. Such a sentiment is as likely to be true in public service agencies as in the private sector.

The only universal axiom to emerge is that the hiving off of marketing or aspects of it, most usually promotion, to independent agencies is likely to exacerbate such a gap, and make partnership more difficult, not only between organisations or economic sectors, but within them.

*The planner as market manager*

Organisations will only be as effective as the people who staff them. In purely practical terms the skills of those practising marketing have been developed in the selling of goods and services by profit-seeking private firms on markets regulated by monetary standards of value. It is not surprising therefore that such expertise is more likely to be found in the private than public sector. The adoption of marketing techniques almost inevitably involves the import of personnel whose experience is primarily in private sector working methods. What can be loosely termed the ethos of the organisation cannot fail to be imported alongside the techniques. At its simplest level most local authority and national or national agency promotion and public relations departments are staffed by individuals whose technical experience, professional associations and career expect-ations lie within the private sector. Cities are in fact being sold by those accustomed to selling soap flakes and are being promoted by public relations specialists whose past, and probably future, tasks are likely to have been the promotion of a brand of cigarettes or chain of hotels. This does not bring into question either their expertise, or integrity in executing public sector commissions. But it does raise a number of problems for town planning. Above all it makes the integration of marketing procedures and public service objectives more difficult.

If marketing is to be part of public sector planning then it must be exercised, or at the very least its capabilities and results understood, by public sector planners. The traditional planner, however, has particularly in Western Europe a pronounced weakness in dealing with the market-place (Knox and Cullen, 1981). What is required is, 'A new kind of expertise more akin to theatrical management than traditional town planning. It needs a peculiar combination of vision, intuition, organisation and determination' (Hall, 1987, p. 130). The flexibility, initiative and opportunism of the entrepreneur must be grafted on to the integrity and professional values of the public servant. The challenge for the planners, and thus those concerned with their education, and re-education, is clear.

There are strongly expressed arguments for and against the introduction of marketing, at whatever level, in public sector management. This is inevitable for all the reasons suggested above, given the far-reaching consequences for organisational structures, methods of accountability and norms of operation within public administrations, as well as being a consequence of the political ideological overtones with which it has become associated. The importance of this debate is obvious. The seriousness of the problems facing cities at the end of the twentieth century are difficult to exaggerate and have been publicly aired in many doom-laden scenarios over the last ten years. The public planning approaches developed in the course of this century have failed to live up to the expectations that both their practitioners and society as a whole expected. Marketing as a new way of viewing cities and thus the problems of their management in the public interest offers a largely unexplored potential. Such an important debate should not be based, as it all too often is, upon either a series of misunderstandings or the propagation of a set of universal panaceas whose mechanistic application guarantees a formula for success. Either route will lead to disillusionment and the failure to realise the potential offered by this opportunity.

# References

Alexander, E.R. (1988), 'The Netherlands Unique Planning System: a visitor's comparison', *Rooilijn*, 5, 145–50.

Allaert, G. (1989a), 'De publieke private samenwerking te Baltimore (USA) en de planologische context', *Planologisch Nieuws*, 9 (1), 34–7.

Allaert, G. (1989b), *Public-private partnerships for the city-region in Flanders* (Managing the Metropolis, University of Salford, Salford).

Allport, G.W. (1954), *The nature of prejudice* (Beacon, Boston).

Alteren, G. van (1989), 'Geweld en onveiligheidsgevoelens in de binnenstad van Groningen' in H. Voogd (ed.), *Stedelijk planning in perspectief* (Geopers, Groningen).

Andriesse, F. (1986), 'City marketing, een onontgonnen terrein', *Tijdschrift van Marketing*, May, 48–9.

Ashworth, G.J. (1988), 'Marketing the historic city for tourism' in B. Goodall and G.J. Ashworth (eds), *Marketing in the Tourism Industry* (Croom Helm, Beckenham).

Ashworth, G.J. and Bergsma, J. (1987) 'New policies for tourism: opportunities or problems', *Tijdschrift voor Economische en Sociale Geografie*, 78 (2), 151–5.

Ashworth, G.J. and de Haan, T.Z. (1986), 'Uses and users of the tourist-historic city', *Field Studies 10* (Faculty of Spatial Sciences, Groningen).

Ashworth, G.J. and de Haan, T.Z. (1987), 'Regionalising the resort system: tourist regions on the Languedoc coast', *Field Studies 6* (Faculty of Spatial Sciences, Groningen).

Ashworth, G.J. and Sijtsma, P. (1990), 'Revitalising the city, some experiences from Ontario and Quebec', *Field Studies 17* (Faculty of Spatial Sciences, Groningen).

Ashworth, G.J. and Voogd, H. (1987), 'The marketing of European heritage as an economic resource' in J.J.M. Angement and A. Bongenaar (eds), *Planning without a passport* (Netherlands Geographical Studies, 44, Amsterdam).

Ashworth, G.J. and Voogd, H. (1988), 'Marketing the city: concepts, processes and Dutch applications', *Town Planning Review*, 59, 65–79.

Ashworth, G.J. and Voogd, H. (1990), 'Can you sell places for tourism?' in G.J. Ashworth and B. Goodall (eds), *Marketing tourism places*, (Routledge, London).

Bahrenberg, G., Fisher, M.M. and Nijkamp, P. (eds) (1984), *Recent developments in spatial data analysis: methodology, measurement, models* (Gower, Aldershot).

Bailey, J.T. (1989), *Marketing cities in the 1980s and beyond*, (American Economic Development Council, Cleveland).

Barke, M. and France, L. (1986), 'The marketing of Spain as a holiday destination', *Tourist Review*, 41 (3), 27–30.

Bartels, C.P.A. and Timmer, M. (1987), *City marketing: instruments and effects* (Paper at the European Regional Science Association, Athens).

Bateman, M. (1986), *Office development: a geographical analysis* (Croom Helm, London).

Batty, M. (1976), *Urban modelling: algorithms, calibrations, predictions* (Cambridge University Press, Cambridge).

Bavoux, P. (1989), 'Art urbaine et espace public à Oullins', *Les Annales de la Recherche, Urbaine Image et Memoires* (Lyon).

Bavoux, P. and Paget, J.P. (1986), *Art public et identite urbaine* (Ministère de l'équipement, du logement, de aménagement du territoire et des transports, Paris).

Beeston, J. (1989), *Birmingham heartlands* (Managing the metropolis, Salford).

Benington, J. (1986), 'Local economic strategies: paradigms for a planned economy', *Local Economy*, 1, 7–24.

Berkers, M., de Boer, G., van Doorn, G., Glas, R., Jense, H., Koopman, K., Oost, L. and Renkema, J. (1986), 'Norwich: policy in a tourist-historic city', *Veldstudies 9* (Faculty of Spatial Sciences, Groningen).

Boogholt, W.J.J. and ter Hark, H.P. (1988), 'De Regionale positie van de gemeente Groningen', *Socio-geografisch Reeks 45* (Faculty of Spatial Sciences, Groningen).

Bourne, L.S. (1975), *Urban systems: strategies for regulation* (Clarendon Press, Oxford).

Bourne, L.S. (1976), 'Housing supply and housing market behaviour in residential development' in D.T. Herbert and R.J. Johnston (eds), *Spatial processes and form* (Wiley, London).

Bouwers, H.J. and Pellenbarg, P.H. (1989), 'Konkurrentie analyse als basis voor city-marketing: een case studie' in H. Voogd (ed.), *Stedelijk planning in perspectief* (Geopers, Groningen).

Brooker-Gross, S.R. (1985), 'The changing concept of place in the news' in J. Burgess and J.R. Gold, *Geography, the media and popular culture* (Croom Helm, Beckenham).

Brooks, H., Liebman, L. and Schelling, C.S. (eds) (1984), *Public-private partnerships: new opportunities for meeting social needs* (Ballinger, Cambridge, Mass.).

Brown, B.J.H. (1985), 'Personal perception and community speculation; a British resort in the nineteenth century', *Annals of tourism research*, 12, 353–69.

Brown, B.J.H. (1988), 'Developments in the promotion of major seaside resorts: how to effect a transition by really making an effort' in B. Goodall and G.J. Ashworth (eds), *Marketing in the tourism industry* (Croom Helm, Beckenham).

Brown, G.M., Charbonneau, J.J. and Hay, M.J. (1978), 'The value of wildlife estimated by the hedonic approach', *Working Paper 6* (US Department of the Interior).

Buck, M. (1988), 'The role of travel agent and tour operator' in B. Goodall and G.J. Ashworth (eds), *Marketing in the tourism industry* (Croom Helm, Beckenham).

Burgess, J. (1974), 'Stereotypes and urban images', *Area*, 6, 167–71.

Burgess, J. (1982), 'Selling places: environmental images for the executive', *Regional Studies*, 16 (1), 1–17.

Burgess, J. (1985), 'News from nowhere: the press, the riots and the myth of the inner city' in J. Burgess and J.R. Gold (eds), *Geography, the media and popular culture* (Croom Helm, Beckenham).

Burgess, J. and Gold, J.R. (1985), *Geography, the media and popular culture* (Croom Helm, Beckenham).

Burgess, J. and Wood, P. (1988), 'Decoding docklands: place advertising and decision making strategies of the small firm' in J. Eyles and D.M. Smith (eds), *Qualitative methods in human geography* (Polity Press, London).

Burtenshaw, D., Bateman, M. and Ashworth, G.J. (1981), *The city in West Europe* (John Wiley, Chichester).

Bussink, F.L. (1988), *Samenwerken bij het ruimtelijk beleid* (Samsom, Alphen aan de Rijn).

Butler, R.W. (1980), 'The concept of a tourism cycle of evolution', *Canadian Geographer*, 24, 5–12.

Buursink, J. (1987), 'Gemeenten en hun beeld' in J.G. Borchert and J. Buursink (eds), *Citymarketing en geografie* (Nederlandse Geografische Studies, 43, 72–92).

Buursink, J. and Borchert, J.G. (eds) (1987), 'Citymarketing en geografie', *Nederlandse Geografische Studies*, 43.

Capon, N. (1981), 'Marketing strategy. Differences between state and privately owned corporations: an explanatory analysis', *Journal of Marketing*, 45, 11–18.

Chapin, F.S. and Kaiser, E.J. (1985) (third revised edition), *Urban land use planning* (University of Illinois Press, Urbana/Chicago).

City of Glasgow (1989), *Perceptions of Glasgow as inward investment location* (Report to the Town Clerk).

Clarke, A. (1985), 'Destination marketing: Gwent county approach', *Tourism Management*, December, 297–301.

Cooke, P. (1987), 'Spatial development processes: organized or disorganized?' in N. Trift and P. Williams (eds), *Class and space: the making of urban society* (Routledge and Kegan, London).

Coste, M. (1989), 'Les images de communication des villes', *Image et Memoires* (Lyon).

Cramwinckel, M. and Nelissen, N. (1989), 'Stedelijk identiteit door de bril van de burger gezien' in N. Nelissen (ed.), *Stedenstrijd: beschouwing over inter en intra urbane rivaliteit* (Kerkebosch, Zeist).

Crompton, J.L. (1979a), 'Motivation for pleasure vacations', *Annals of Tourism Research*, 6, 408–24.

Crompton, J.L. (1979b), 'An assessment of the image of Mexico as a vacation destination', *Journal of Travel Research*, 17 (4), 18–23.

Dann, G. (1976), 'The holiday was simply fantastic', *Tourism Review*, 31 (5), 19–23.

Dann, G. (1978), 'Tourist satisfaction: a highly complex variable', *Annals of Tourism Research*, 4, 440–3.

Dann, G. (1981), 'Tourist motivation: an appraisal', *Annals of Tourism Research*, 8, 187–219.

DATAR (1989), *Les villes Européennes* (La Documentation Française, Paris).

Davidoff, P. (1965), 'Advocacy and pluralism planning', *Journal of the American Institute of Planners*, 31, 331–9.

Davies, R.L. (1976), *Marketing geography* (Retail and Planning Associates, Cambridge).

Davis, P. (ed.) (1986), *Public-private partnerships: improving urban life* (The Academy of Political Science and New York City Partnership, New York).

De Decker, P. (1989), 'Ruimtelijke planning en public-private partnerships: een "Dangerous liaison"?', *Planologisch Nieuws*, 9 (3), 28–46.

Department of the Environment (1987), *Inner city programmes 1987–1993*.

Desfors, G., Goldrick, M. and Merrens, R. (1988), 'Redevelopment on the North American Waterfront: the case of Toronto' in B.S. Hoyle, D.A. Pinter and M.S. Husain (eds), *Revitalising the waterfront* (Belhaven, London).

Dietvorst, A. (1987), *Beeldvorming en keuze van vakantiegebieden in Nederland* (Werkgroep Recreatie en toerisme, KUN, Nijmegen).

Dilley, R.S. (1986), 'Tourist brochures and tourist images', *Canadian Geographer*, 30, 59–65.

Dijkstra, J.B. (1989), *Provincie en publiek-private samenwerking* (PPD-Groningen/ Rijksuniversiteit Groningen, Groningen).

Doorn, A.J.L. van (1986), *Stadspromotie tussen slogan en sukses* (Reklarijn Bureau, Arnhem).

Downs, R.M. and Stea, D. (1973), *Image and environment* (Aldine, New York).

Dijk, R. van (1990), 'Comparative tourism images of Egypt' in G.J. Ashworth, R. van Dijk and P. Laban (eds), *Images, markets and place products: East Mediterranean tourism destinations* (Onderzoekverslagen, Groningen).

Dunning, J.H. and Norman, G. (1987), 'Location choice of offices of international companies', *Environment and Planning*, A 19, 613–31.

Dutton, W.H. and Kraemer, K.R. (1985), *Modelling as negotiating: the political dynamics of computer models in the policy process* (Ablex Press, Norwood, NJ).

Dyckman, J.W. (1961), 'What makes planners plan?', *Journal of the American Institute of Planners*, 27, 163–70.

Eldridge, J.E.T. (1971), *Systems analysis and individual behaviour, in Sociology and industrial life* (Michael Joseph, London).

Eisenberg, R. and Englander, D.W. (1987), 'The best places to live in America', *Money*, August, 16, 34–44.

Falk, N. (1986), 'Baltimore and Lowell: two American approaches', *Built Environment*, 12 (3), 145–52.

Faludi, A. (1973), *Planning theory* (Pergamon, Oxford).

Faludi, A. (1987), *A decision centred view of environmental planning* (Pergamon, Oxford).

Fines, S.H. (1981), *The marketing of ideas and social issues* (Praeger, New York).

Fostler, R.S. and Berger, R.A. (eds) (1982), *Public-private partnership in American cities* (Lexington Books, Lexington, Mass.).

Friedman, M. (1970), 'The social responsibility of business is to increase its profits', *New York Times*, 30 September, 33.

Friedmann, J. (1973), *Retracking America: a theory of transactive planning* (Anchor Press, New York).

Friedmann, J. (1989), 'Planning, politics, and the environment', *Journal of the*

American Planning Association, 55 (3), 334–41.

Friend, J.K. and Jessop, W.N. (1969), *Local government and strategic choice* (Tavistock, London).

Friend, J.K., Power, J.M. and Yewlett, C.J. (1974), *Public planning: the inter-corporate dimension* (Tavistock, London).

Gaedeke, R.M. (1977), *Marketing in private and public non–profit organisations: perspectives and illustrations* (Goodyear, Santa Monica).

Galbraith, J.K. (1967), *The new industrial state* (Hamish Hamilton, London).

Gault, M. (1989), *Villes intermédiaires pour L'Europe* (Syros, Paris).

Gent, A.P. van (1984), 'City marketing en de gevechten om binnen en buitenlandse investeerders', *Tijdschrift van Marketing*, December, 10–15.

Gilbert, N. and Specht, H. (1977), *Dynamics of community planning* (Ballinger, Cambridge, Mass.).

Gitelson, R.J. and Crompton, J.L. (1983), 'The planning horizons and sources of information used by pleasure vacationers', *Journal of Travel Research*, 21 (3), 2–7.

Gold, J.R. (1985), 'From metropolis to the city' in J. Burgess and J.R. Gold (eds), *Geography, the media and popular culture* (Croom Helm, Beckenham).

Goodall, B. (1988), 'How tourists choose their holidays: an analytical framework' in B. Goodall and G.J. Ashworth (eds), *Marketing in the tourism industry: the promotion of destination regions* (Croom Helm, Beckenham).

Goodey, B. (1968), *A pilot study of the geographical perception of North Dakota students* (Department of Geography, University of North Dakota, Grand Forks).

Goodey, B. (1974), 'Images of place: essays on environmental perception, communication and education', *Occasional Papers*, 30 (Centre for Urban and Regional Studies, Birmingham).

Gould, P. and Lyew-Ayee, A. (1985), 'Television in the third world: a high wind on Jamaica' in J. Burgess and J.R. Gold, *Geography, the media and popular culture* (Croom Helm, Beckenham).

Gould, P. and White, R. (1974), *Mental maps* (Penguin, Harmondsworth).

Green, C. (1989), *The Manchester, Salford, Trafford Integrated Development Operation: a programme for regeneration* (Managing the Metropolis, Salford).

Gulliver, S. (1989), *National agency strategy: the experience of the Scottish Development Agency* (Managing the Metropolis, Salford).

Gunsteren, H.R. van (1976), *The quest for control* (Wiley, New York).

Gwinner, R.F., Brown, S.W., Hagan, A.J., Ostrom, L.L., Rowe, K.L., Schlachter, J.L., Schmidt, A.H. and Schrok, D.L. (1977), *Marketing: an environmental perspective* (West, St Paul).

Haan, T.Z. de, Ashworth, G.J. and Stabler, M. (1990), 'The tourist destination as product: the case of Languedoc' in G.J. Ashworth and B. Goodall (eds), *Marketing tourism places* (Routledge, London).

Habermas, J. (1973), *Legitimationsprobleme im spaetkapitalismus* (Suhrkamp, Frankfurt am Main).

Haddon, J. (1960), 'A view of foreign lands', *Geography*, 45, 286–9.

Hall, E.T. (1969), *The hidden dimension* (Andov, New York).

Hall, P. (1987), 'Urban development and the future of tourism', *Tourism Management*, 8 (2), 129–30.

Harrison, J. and Sarre, P. (1978), 'Personal construct theory in the measurement of environmental images: problems and methods', *Enviroment and Behaviour*, 3, 351–71.

Hart, M. and Harrison, R.T. (1990), *Inward investment and economic change* (Institute of British Geographers, Annual Conference, Glasgow).

Hart, R. (1984), 'Geography of children – children's geography' in T.F. Saarinen, D. Saarinen and J.L. Sell (eds), *Environmental perception and behaviour* (University of Chicago, Geography Research Papers 209, 99–129).

Harvey, D. (1988), 'Flexible accumulation through urbanization: reflections on "post-modernism" in the American city', *Antipode*, 19, 3, 260–86.

Harvey, D. (1989), *The urban experience* (Blackwell, Oxford).

Hawes, J.M., Lewison, D.M. and Prough, G.E. (1985), 'The importance of government sponsored location incentives for distribution facilities', *International Journal of Physical Distribution and Materials Management*, 15, 61–9.

Heida, H. and Gordijn, H. (1978), *Regionale woonvoorkeuren* (Planologisch Studiecentrum TNO, Delft).

Hickling, A. (1974), *Managing decisions* (Mantec, Rugby).

Hodge, G. (1985), 'The roots of Canadian planning', *Journal of American Planning Association*, 51 (1), 8–23.

Holcomb, B. (1990), *Revisioning place: de- and re-constructing the image of the industrial city*. Paper presented at the IBG, Glasgow.

Hommes, J. and Geraads, S. (1984), 'Marketing als beleidsvorm', *B & O Cahiers* (VUGA, The Hague).

Hopkins, L.D. (1977), 'Methods for generating land suitability maps: a comparative evaluation', *Journal of the American Institute of Planners*, 43 (4), 386–400.

Hoyle, B.S., Pinder, D.A. and Husain, M.S. (eds) (1988), *Revitalising the waterfront: international dimensions of dockland development* (Belhaven, London).

Hunt, J.D. (1975), 'Image as factor in tourism development', *Journal of Travel Research*, 13 (3), 1–7.

Janssen, B.J.P. and Machielse, S. (1988), *Logistiek, ruimtelijke organisatie en infrastructuur* (INRO-TNO, Delft).

Jarvis, B. (1985), 'The truth is only known to guttersnipes' in J. Burgess and J.R. Gold, *Geography, the media and popular culture* (Croom Helm, Beckenham).

Jefferson, A. and Lickorish, L. (1988), *Marketing tourism: a practical guide* (Longmans, London).

Jong, M.W. de and Lambooy, J.G. (1986), 'Modelstad Baltimore', *Intermediair*, 22, 43–9.

Jossip, B., Bonnet, K., Bromley, S. and Ling, T. (1987), 'Popular capitalism, flexible accumulation and left strategy', *New Left Review*, 165, 104–22.

Jowett, G.S. and O'Donnell, V. (1986), *Propaganda and Persuasion* (Sage, Beverly Hills).

Kane, J.N. and Alexander, G.L. (1965), *Nicknames of cities and states of the United States* (Scarecrow, New York).

Kent, P. (1990), 'People, places and priorities: opportunity sets and consumers holiday choice' in G.J. Ashworth and B. Goodall (eds), *Marketing tourism places* (Routledge, London).

Klaassen, L.H., van de Berg, L. and van de Meer, J. (eds) (1989), *The city: engine behind economic recovery* (Avebury, Aldershot).

Kok, J., Offerman, G. and Pellenbarg, P. (1985), 'Innovatieve bedrijven in het grootschaalig milieu', *Sociaal-geografisch Reeks*, 34 (Faculty of Spatial Sciences, Groningen).

Kotler, P. (1972), 'A generic concept of marketing', *Journal of Marketing*, April, 46–54.

Kotler, P. (1982), *Marketing for non-profit organisations* (Prentice Hall, Englewood Cliffs).

Kotler, P. (1986) (3rd edn), *Principles of marketing* (Prentice Hall, Englewood Cliffs).

Kotler, P. and Levy, S.J. (1969), 'Broadening the concept of marketing', *Journal of Marketing*, January, 10–15.

Kotler, P. and Zaltman, G. (1971), 'Social marketing: an approach to planned social change', *Journal of Marketing*, July, 3–12.

Knox, P. and Cullen, J. (1981), 'The planner as urban manager: an exploration of the attitudes and self-image of senior British planners', *Environment and Planning*, A 13, 886–98.

Lancaster, K.J. (1966), 'A new approach to consumer theory', *Journal of Political Economy*, 84, 132–57.

Langenieux-Villard, P. (1985), *L'information municipale* (Presses Universitaires de France, Paris).

Lawless, P. (1986), *The evolution of spatial policy* (Pion, London).

Lazer, W. and Kelley, E.J. (1973), *Social marketing: perspectives and view points* (Irwin, London).

Lee, D.B. (1973), 'Requiem for large-scale models', *Journal of the American Institute of Planners*, 31 (2), 158–65.

Lemstra, W. (1987), 'Public-private partnership', *Economisch Statistische Berichten*, 72 (3607), 514–17.

Lever, W. (1987), 'Policy for the post-industrial city' in B. Robson (ed.), *Managing the city* (Croom Helm, Beckenham).

Leven, C.L. and Stover, M.E. (1989), *Advances in Rating the Quality of Life in Urban Areas*. Paper presented at the 29th European Congress Regional Science Association, Cambridge (UK).

Lindblom, C.E. (1964), 'The science of "muddling through"' in W.J. Gore and J.W. Dyson (eds), *The making of decisions* (Free Press, New York).

Lovelock, C.H. and Weinberg, C.B. (1984), *Marketing for public and non-profit managers* (Wiley, New York).

Lovelock, C.H., Lewin, G., Day, G.S. and Bateson, J.E.G. (1987), *Marketing public transit: a strategic approach* (Praeger, New York).

Lowenthal, D. (1961), 'Geography, experience and imagination: towards a geographical epistemology', *Annals of Association of American Geographers*, 51, 241–66.

Lukkes, P. (1988a), 'Investeren in binnensteden', *Onderzoek en Advies*, 39 (Faculteit der Ruimtelijk Wetenschappen, Groningen).

Lukkes, P. (1988b), 'De beste plek', *Onderzoek en Advies*, 43 (Faculteit der Ruimtelijk Wetenschappen, Groningen).

Lynch, K. (1960), *Image of the city* (MIT Press, Cambridge, Mass.).

McLoughlin, J.B. (1969), *Urban and regional planning* (Faber and Faber, London).

Meester, W.J. and Pellenbarg, P. (1986), 'Subjektieve waardering van bedrijfs-vestigingsmilieus in Nederland', *Sociaal-Geografische Reeks*, 39 (GIRUG, Groningen).

Mercer, D. (1971), 'Discretionary travel', *Australian Geographical Studies*, 9, 133–43.

Middleton, V.T.C. (1988), *Marketing in travel and tourism* (Heinemann, London).

Milgram, S. and Jodelet, D. (1976), 'Psychological maps of Paris' in H. Prashamsky (ed.), *Environmental psychology* (Rinehart Holt and Winston, New York).

Miller, D.H. (1985), 'Equity and efficiency effects of investment decisions' in A. Faludi and H. Voogd (eds), *Evaluation of complex policy problems* (DUP, Delft).

Miller, D.H. (1989), *Developing the local economy – the local authority role* (Managing the Metropolis, University of Salford).

Miller, D.H. (1990), 'The organizational and political environments of planning evaluation' in D. Shefer and H. Voogd (eds), *Evaluation methods for urban and regional plans* (Pion, London).

Molotoch, H. (1976), 'The city as a growth machine', *American Journal of Sociology*, 82, 309–32.

Monheim, H. (1972), 'Zur Attraktivitat Deutscher Stade', *Berichte zur Regionalforsch*, 8.

Montalieu, J.P. (1989), 'Les macarons sur les automobiles', *Annales de la Recherche Urbaine, Image et Memoires* (Lyon).

Muller, N. and Needham, B. (eds) (1989), *Ruimtelijk handelen* (Kerckebosch, Zeist).

Murphy, P.E. (1985), *Tourism: a community approach* (Methuen, London).

NBT (1986), *Imago studie Nederland* (Nationaal Bureau voor Toerisme, Leidschendam).

Neisser, V. (1976), *Cognition and reality: principles and implications of cognitive psychology* (Freeman, San Francisco).

Nelissen, N. (ed.) (1989), *Stedenstrijd: beschowing over inter en intra urbane rivaliteit* (Kerkebosch, Zeist).

Neven, J.R. and Houston, M.J. (1980), 'Image as a central component of attraction to intraurban shopping areas', *Journal of Retailing*, 56, 77–93.

Nijkamp, P., Leitner, H. and Wrigley, N. (eds) (1985), *Measuring the unmeasurable* (Martinus Nijhoff, Dordrecht).

Nolan, D.S. (1976), 'Tourist use and evaluation of travel information sources', *Journal of Travel Research*, 14, 6–8.

Nott, P.C. (1984), 'A strategic planning network for non-profit organisation', *Strategic Management Journal*, 5, 57–75.

Pattinson, G. (1990), 'Place promotion by tourist boards: the example of "beautiful Berkshire"' in G.J. Ashworth and B. Goodall (eds), *Marketing tourism places* (Routledge, London).

Pearce, D.G. (1981), *Tourist development* (Longmans, London).

Pearce, P.L. (1977), 'Mental souvenirs: a study of tourists and their city maps', *Australian Journal of Psychology*, 29, 203–10.

Pearce, P.L. (1981a), *The social psychology of tourist behaviour* (Pergamon, Oxford).

Pearce, P.L. (1981b), 'Perceived changes in holiday destinations: an illustration of the grid approach', *Annals of Tourism Research*, 8.

Peelen, E.J. (1987), 'City marketing', *Vastgoed*, 3, 96–8.

Penny, J.R. (1989), *OECD and EC policy, investment strategies and economic regeneration* (Managing the Metropolis, Salford).

Pellenbarg, P.H. (1985), 'Bedrijfsrelokatie en ruimtelijke kognitie', *Sociaal-Geografische Reeks* (Faculty of Spatial Sciences, Groningen).
Pellenbarg, P., Popken, B., Raggers, G., Sijtsma, P. and Voogd, H. (1988), *De markt positie van Hoogeveen* (Geopers, Groningen).
Pinch, S. (1985), *Cities and services: the geography of collective consumption* (Routledge and Kegan Paul, London).
Pocock, D.C.D. (ed.) (1981), *Humanistic geography and literature: essays on the experience of place* (Croom Helm, London).
Pocock, D. and Hudson, R. (1978), *Images of the urban environment* (Macmillan, London).
Popper, F. (1981), 'Siting LULUS', *Planning*, 47 (4), 12–15.
Pressman, J.L. and Wildavsky, A.B. (1973), *Implementations* (University of California Press, Berkeley).
Pumain, D. (1989), *City image in an urban system*. Paper at the 29th European Congress of the Regional Science (mimeographed).
RPD (Rijksplanologische Dienst) (1986), *Ruimtelijke verkenning infrastructuur* (Den Haag).
RPD (Rijksplanologische Dienst) (1987), *Ruimtelijke perspectieven* (Den Haag).
RPD (Rijksplanologische Dienst) (1988), *Vierde nota over de ruimtelijke ordening ('Fourth Report'), deel a, Staatsuitgeverij* (Den Haag).
Raaij, F. van (1984), 'Vacation decisions, activities and satisfactions', *Annals of Tourism Research*, 11, 101–13.
Raaij, F. van (1986), 'Consumer research on tourism: mental and behavioural constructs', *Annals of Tourism Research*, 13, 1–10.
Racine, P. (1980), *Le mission impossible?* (Midi Libre, Montpellier).
Rados, D.L. (1981), *Marketing for non-profit organisations* (Auburn House, Boston).
Raggers, G.G. (1989), 'Revitalisering: nieuwe stimulansen voor de bestaande stad' in H. Voogd (ed.), *Stedelijk planning in perspectief* (Geopers, Groningen).
Raggers, G.G. and Voogd, H. (1989), 'Investeren in planvorming', *Planologische Discussiebijdragen 1989*, part II, 555–64.
Rand-McNally (1985), *Places rated almanac* (Rand-McNally Publishers, Skokie, Ill.).
Rao, S. and Farley, J.U. (1987), 'Effects of environmental perceptions and cognitive complexity on search and information processing', *Psychology and Marketing*, 4 (4), 288–301.
Rapoport, A. (1982), *The meaning of the built environment: a non-verbal communication approach* (Sage, Beverly Hills).
Rietveld, P. (1984), 'The use of qualitative information in macro-economic policy analysis' in M. Despontin, P. Nijkamp and J. Spronk (eds), *Macro-economic policy planning with conflicting goals* (Springer, Berlin).
Riley, S. and Palmer, J. (1976), 'Of attitudes and latitudes: a repertory grid study of perception of seaside resorts' in P. Slater (ed.), *Explorations of interpersonal space* (Wiley, London).
Roloff, M.E. and Miller, G.R. (eds) (1980), *Persuasion: new directions in theory and research* (Sage, Beverly Hills).
Rugg, D.D. (1971), *The demand for foreign travel*, unpublished Ph.D. thesis, University of California, Los Angeles.
Saarinen, T.F. (1973), 'Student views of the world' in R.M. Downs and D. Stea

(eds), *Image and environment* (Arnold, London).

Saarinen, T.F., Seamon, D. and Sell, J.R. (1984), 'Environmental perception and behaviour: an inventory and prospect', *Geographical Research Papers*, 209 (University of Chicago).

Sadler, D. (1990), *Place marketing: competitive places and the construction of hegemony in Britain in the 1980s*. Paper presented at the Institute of British Geographers Annual Conference, Glasgow.

Saunders, P. (1986) (2nd edn), *Social theory and the urban question* (Hutchinson, London).

Schmoll, G.A. (1977), *Tourism promotion* (Tourism International Press, London).

Schudson, M. (1984), *Advertising: the uneasy persuasion* (Basic Books, New York).

Shefer, D. and Voogd, H. (eds) (1990), *Evaluation methods for urban and regional plans* (Pion Ltd, London).

Short, J. (1989), *The humane city* (Blackwell, Oxford).

Sierra Magazine (1986), 'The best and worst American cities', *Sierra*, 71, 2, 19.

Sliepen, W. (1988), *Marketing van de historische omgeving* (Netherlands Research Institute for Tourism, Breda).

Stabler, M.J. (1988), 'The image of destination regions' in B. Goodall and G.J. Ashworth (eds), *Marketing in the tourism industry* (Croom Helm, London).

Steiss, A.W. (1974), *Models for the analysis and planning of urban systems* (Lexington Books, Lexington, Mass.).

Stoker, G. (1989), 'Policy review section: urban development corporations, a review', *Regional Studies*, 23 (2), 159–73.

Tolman, E. (1948), 'Cognitive maps in rats and men', *Psychology Review*, 55, 189–208.

Toronto Harbourfront Corporation (1988), *Annual Report* (Toronto).

Triandis, H.C. (1977), *Interpersonal behavior* (Brooks/Cole, Monterey).

Tuan, Y.F. (1974), *Topophilia: a study of environmental perception, attitudes and values* (Prentice Hall, Englewood Cliffs, NJ).

Tuan, Y.F. (1975), 'Images and mental maps', *Annals, Association of American Geographers*, 65, 205–13.

Uzzell, D. (1984), 'An alternative structuralist approach to the psychology of tourism marketing', *Annals of Tourism Research*, 11, 79–100.

Veen, W. van der and Voogd, H. (1987), *Gemeentepromotie en bedrijfsac-quisitie* (Geopers, Groningen).

Voogd, H. (1982), 'Issues and tendencies in Dutch regional planning' in R. Hudson and J. Lewis (eds), *Regional planning in Europe* (Pion, London).

Voogd, H. (1983), *Multicriteria evaluation for urban and regional planning* (Pion, London).

Voogd, H. (1987a), 'Groningen: van regelplanning naar prikkelplanning', *Contour*, 4, 14–17.

Voogd, H. (1987b), *Qualitative and quantitative spatial potency analysis: the program POTENT* (Department of Urban and Regional Planning, University of Groningen, Netherlands).

Voogd, H. (1988), 'Van regelplanning naar prikkelplanning: een moeilijke opgave' in P.M. Blok (ed.), *Colloquium Vervoersplanologisch Speurwerk*

1988 – Nederland in nota's, strategie en pragmatisme in beleid en onderzoek, part 1, 233–48 (Delft).

Voogd, H. (1989a), 'City-management en city-marketing: de nieuwe zakelijkheid in planologenland', *Planologisch Nieuws*, 9 (1), 22–5.

Voogd, H. (1989b), 'Profilering van de stad voor investeerders', *Economisch Statistische Berichten*, 74 (3722), 840–50.

Voogd, H. and Wijk, W. van der (1989), 'Recreatieve imagos en gemeentelijk voorlichting' in H. Voogd (ed.), *Stedelijk planning in perspectief* (Geopers, Groningen).

WTO (World Tourism Organisation) (1985), *Identification and evaluation of those components of tourism services which have a bearing on tourist satisfaction* (WTO, Madrid).

Walker, J.D. (1976), 'Using research to develop and test advertising for a destination', *Proceedings Travel Research Association*, 171–4.

Walmesley, D.J. (1988), *Urban living: the individual in the city* (Longmans, London).

Weber, M. (1947), *The theory of social and economic organisation* (Henderson and Talcott Parsons, London).

Weiss, M.A. (1989), 'Planning history: what story? what meaning? what future?', *Journal of the American Planning Association*, 55 (1), 82–4.

White, L.D. (1926), *Introduction to the study of public administration* (MacMillan, New York).

Wildavsky, A. (1964), *The politics of the budgetary process* (Little Brown, Boston).

Wilson, A.G. (1974), *Urban and regional models in geography and planning* (Wiley, Chichester).

Wyatt, R. (1989), *Intelligent planning* (Unwin Hyman, London).

Young, K. and Mason, C. (eds) (1983), *Urban economic development: new roles and relationships* (MacMillan, London).

Young, S., Leland, O. and Fergin, B. (1978), 'Some practical considerations in market segmentation', *Journal of Marketing*, 15, 405–12.

Zandvoort, H. van (1989), 'Samenwerking tussen gemeentelijke overheid en project ontwikkelaars' in N. Nelissen (ed.), *Stedenstrijd: beschouwing over inter en intra urbane rivaliteit* (Kerkebosch, Zeist).

# Author index

# Subject index

198